The Reconstruction Era

A Captivating Guide to a Period in the History of the United States of America That Greatly Impacted American Civil Rights after the War for Southern Independence

Free Bonus from Captivating History (Available for a Limited time)

Hi History Lovers!

Now you have a chance to join our exclusive history list so you can get your first history ebook for free as well as discounts and a potential to get more history books for free! Simply visit the link below to join.

Captivatinghistory.com/ebook

Also, make sure to follow us on Facebook, Twitter and Youtube by searching for Captivating History.

Contents

Prologue: The Whispers of War

Before we begin to explore the Reconstruction Era, let's look more closely at the causes of the Civil War and the events leading up to the war's first action. The situation in the United States when Abraham Lincoln was elected to the presidency can only be described as a tinder box waiting to explode in flames. There were many issues between the populous North, whose economy was thriving due to the rising industries, and the South, whose economy was based on millions of slaves. Although Northerners could be quite prejudiced, the Northern states abolished slavery by 1804. Besides their difference in opinions when it came to slavery, the Southerners also resented what they saw as unfair taxation from the federal government and the denial of states' rights.

There was also another major issue facing the Union: what to do with the new territories. Of course, each side wanted the new states that were admitted to the Union to coincide with their beliefs on slavery. The Missouri Compromise of 1820 helped placate the people for a time, but the Kansas-Nebraska Act of 1854 rekindled tensions, culminating in "Bleeding Kansas," which was essentially a civil war within Kansas. Some refer to it as the overture to the Civil War.

Abraham Lincoln, a Republican, was elected as the sixteenth president in 1860. While Lincoln ran on a platform that called for the limitation of slavery, he did not seek to dismantle the institution in states where it already existed because the practice of slavery was supported by the Constitution. However, the South feared that this would change and that Lincoln would approve of policies that would eventually dismantle slavery while favoring the business practices of the North.

The Southerners were not entirely wrong, as Lincoln favored the benefits that came from the Industrial Revolution. Unfortunately, these benefits did not flow below the Mason-Dixon line (the informal boundary line between the free North and the slave states in the South). The Industrial Revolution never really took off in the agricultural South, as 90 percent of the country's manufacturing economy was in the North by 1860.

The South mainly depended on the cotton trade, which grew exponentially with the invention of the cotton gin. Most of their cotton was exported; in fact, the South produced two-thirds of the world's cotton during this time. With this boom in the cotton trade came the demand for more slaves. It also increased the disparity between the whites in the South, as few ever became rich enough to own a large plantation that employed many slaves. Yet despite their monetary differences, white Southerners managed to hold onto the same belief that slavery was advantageous for all and that the blacks who toiled in the fields were lesser than they were.

So even though the South lagged far behind the North on the industrial side of things, it was not all bleak for the South when the Civil War broke out. The South had tremendous wealth in the slave-run economy. In 1860, slaves were worth more than all of the North's banks, factories, and railroads combined. Cotton was also a worldwide export crop, which led the Confederate leaders to expect economic, military, and diplomatic assistance in the war from European countries. Although the North had an estimated 3.5 million able-bodied men in comparison to the South's 1 million men (excluding slaves), the Southerners had much more experience in fighting. But perhaps most important of all, the Southerners were united in their beliefs. Not all Northerners were invested enough in the issue of slavery to go to war and die for people who they saw as inferior. It is possible these factors led to overconfidence in the Confederacy.

On December 20th, 1860, South Carolina officially seceded from the United States. Other states started to follow suit, and before Lincoln was inaugurated in March 1861, seven states had seceded the Union. These seven states established the Confederate States of America in February 1861, and little over a month later, the South would attack Fort Sumter, signaling the beginning of the Civil War.

Introduction

After the Civil War ended in 1865, there was much that needed to be addressed. The rights of the freed blacks, how to incorporate those Southern states that reentered the Union, and the economy, among many other issues, all had to be evaluated.

The Reconstruction era sought to fix these issues and lay down the groundwork for a better tomorrow. However, while the government managed to unite the country once again, it failed to solve the crisis that blacks faced in the South and in the country as a whole. One could draw a direct line from the Reconstruction's failure in this arena to the racism in America today.

But what caused it to fail? What is the legacy of the Reconstruction in America today? Together, we will walk along the road from Washington, DC, to Mississippi. We will journey from Lincoln's idealist vision of putting the Union back together to Andrew Johnson's Reconstruction policies to the election of 1876. During this time, three constitutional amendments were passed in about five years. That is quite a feat. And in the midst of passing these amendments, Congress also passed the Civil Rights Act of 1866, the Reconstruction Act of 1867, the Ku Klux Klan Act, and the Civil Rights Act of 1875. However, the election of 1876 effectively ended both the Reconstruction and Lincoln's dream of an America "filled with our better angels."

There were some good things that came from the Reconstruction, such as public schools for African Americans, the end of slavery, and the African Americans' right to vote. Blacks could own property and enter into contracts. However, these laws were great on paper, but they didn't meet their full potential in reality.

The good was met with the bad. In response to the Union's integration of blacks into the nation, the South passed restrictive laws known as the Black Codes in 1865 and 1866. This behavior led to the emergence of the Radical Republicans, who believed the abolition of slavery didn't go far enough. These Republicans pushed for even more equitable reforms.

Since the civil rights movement of the 1960s, we have celebrated every "first" black governor, black congressman, black senator, and black state legislators. The truth is there were a number of African Americans in state legislatures and even in Congress between 1867 and the end of the Reconstruction. In the years that followed, white Southerners drove them out with the implementation of the Jim Crow laws and voter suppression tactics. The civil rights movement didn't introduce these "radical ideas" of African Americans holding office. During the Reconstruction, black legislators not only existed—they flourished. Blacks holding public office was fairly common until the Ku Klux Klan's rebirth drove blacks back into living under a second-class status.

After examining the events and milestones of the Reconstruction, there will be a short review of the Supreme Court 1896 doctrine of "separate but equal" in the landmark case of *Plessy v. Ferguson*. This decision stood for decades, and it short-changed thousands of children of color in their education.

At the end of the day, the failure of the Reconstruction was not in the legislation and amendments. It was in the implementation or rather non-implementation of these laws. The country's leaders wanted to obtain their political goals, and in the process, they sacrificed important policies that would have benefited the freed blacks.

Chapter 1 – The Civil War

The year is 1865. America had been tearing itself apart for four years by this point. For many decades before the war broke out, the Northern and Southern states had argued intensely over three essential points. These were slavery, westward expansion, and states' rights in a time of a growing federal government.

When Abraham Lincoln won the presidency in 1860, these arguments boiled over. Initially, there were only seven states in the Confederate States of America, but by May 1861, there were eleven states. However, Lincoln was determined to hold the Union together without losing any state permanently to the Confederacy.

Jefferson Davis became the president of the Confederate States of America, with Alexander Stephens as the vice president. Davis was a war veteran, and he also served as the secretary of war from 1853 to 1857. Stephens was a Georgia representative, and he made what is known as the Cornerstone Speech in 1861. In this speech, Stephens introduced the Confederate Constitution and proclaimed that white supremacy was the "cornerstone" of the Confederacy. He stated that the "peculiar institution of African slavery was the immediate cause of the late rupture [of the Union] and present revolution."

Like most of the other Southerners, Stephens did not believe that "all men are created equal," as the United States Constitution declared. He thought that "those ideas...were fundamentally wrong." Stephens proclaimed, "The foundations are laid, its cornerstone rests, upon the great truth that the negro is not equal to the white man." Stephens firmly believed that for "Black Americans, slavery subordination to the superior race is his natural and normal condition."

Stephens made it very clear in his speech that the continuation and expansion of slavery was the cause of the secession and the war itself. And he was certainly not the only one to think so. For example, when Mississippi seceded, their declaration stated, "Our position is thoroughly identified with the institution of slavery—the greatest material interest of the world." In other words, Mississippi announced that saving the institution of slavery justified a civil war. Their declaration of secession went on to say, "Its labor supplies the product which constitutes by far the largest and most important portions of the commerce of the earth...A blow at slavery is a blow at commerce and civilization."

However, not everyone in the South felt this way, or at least they were not willing to separate from the Union over their beliefs on the matter. A great example of this can be seen in the case of West Virginia. In 1861, Virginia voted on whether or not to secede. Many in the northwestern part of Virginia voted against the referendum. They broke away from the main state of Virginia, which seceded from the Union. In 1863, West Virginia was officially declared a state. It became a critical border state, and it was one of two states admitted to the Union during the Civil War, with the other one being Nevada. However, not everyone was happy with statehood, as there were many slave owners in the southern part of West Virginia. In a way, the conflict in Virginia was a microcosm of the nationwide conflict.

There were a lot of famous battles and figures that arose during the Civil War, but this book is only going to provide a brief description of its end. In 1864, Major General Ulysses S. Grant was appointed as the Union Army's lieutenant general. This decision was perhaps one of the most important of the war. Between Grant and General William Tecumseh Sherman, the Union Army was able to put the Confederate troops on the run and force a surrender. Grant's nine-month siege of Petersburg led to Confederate General Robert E. Lee's retreat. During those nine months, Sherman led his infamous "March to the Sea," during which he burned much of Georgia to the ground. South Carolina fell to Sherman in February 1865, followed by North Carolina. Following the siege on Petersburg, Grant pursued Lee's forces to Appomattox, where Lee surrendered to him.

Unfortunately, Abraham Lincoln was assassinated before the Confederate States of America officially surrendered (however, it should be noted that the war was effectively over once Lee surrendered). John Wilkes Booth, a Southern sympathizer, took matters into his own hands on the fateful day of April 14th, shooting the president while he was enjoying a play. On May 9th, 1865, the Civil War came to a close.

It was a very unfortunate turn of events when President Lincoln was assassinated. The South's strong feelings against Lincoln led Booth to decide it was his duty to eliminate the president. There is little doubt among historians that if Lincoln had lived, the Reconstruction would have been very different. Perhaps there would have been more healing and better relationships between the people.

The Civil War lasted about four years and took the lives of between 616,000 and 1.5 million soldiers. The North proved victorious in the end, so new states added to the Union could no longer even consider implementing slavery. However, war comes with a price, and this price was most certainly felt in the South, as it was essentially a wasteland at the end of the war.

The North won the war for many reasons, but the economic changes it implemented and its burgeoning industrial economy were significant factors. The agricultural and slave-driven economy of the South could not produce the supplies, weapons, and support that the North could. It also could not compete with the manpower of the North.

President Andrew Johnson, who took over after Lincoln was assassinated, would reunite the Union after the South's surrender. Still, much bitterness remains to this day. The South saw its economy destroyed and its land and the families who inhabited it devasted. Union forces had burned the cities of the South to the ground, and there was widespread hunger and homelessness. This bitterness would live on in the oppression of freed blacks in the South.

However, there was just as much bitterness on the part of the North toward the South. For many in the North, slavery was a moral abomination. The thought that the South had killed their president was embedded in Northern attitudes. Still, the Union attempted to show mercy to the Confederate Army, imprisoning few and only executing one.

The South's bitterness only increased, though, and it was fortified by the punishing and humiliating Reconstruction. Thousands of Southerners lost all of their savings and income when the war ended, as the Confederacy's currency and government securities were suddenly without value.

The scene was set for the Reconstruction era, which had lasting effects on the United States of America. As the post-war era began, the South was already suffering from a very shaky economy. The Emancipation Proclamation of 1862, which freed the slaves in the Confederate states, helped to wipe out the unpaid labor force in the South, causing both economic and philosophical pain and anger.

The Emancipation Proclamation was not the only legislation passed during the war that allowed the Union to increase its economic and military advantages. Six essential pieces of legislation were passed during the Civil War: the Homestead Act, the Morrill Act (also known as the Land-Grant College Act), the Pacific Railway Act, the Legal Tender Act, the Internal Revenue Act, and the National Bank Act. To better understand the position the North was in at the end of the war, it is necessary to take a deeper look into these acts.

The Homestead Act

Since the early 1840s, Congress had debated the ideas behind the Homestead Act. This legislature was very popular in the North, but the Southern politicians were skeptical and worried that new territory would be free of slavery. The Homestead Act was finally passed once the Southern delegation had departed the Union in May of 1862.

The Homestead Act offered 160 acres to anyone willing to move to the West. The main condition for receiving this land was that it had to be improved upon, as the US government wanted to foster growth in the Western territories. The passage of this act allowed free white farmers, as well as freed blacks, to make their living off the land, blocking the large plantation owners of the South from expanding and utilizing slaves to work in the fields.

The Morrill Act (the Land-Grant College Act)

This act, which was passed in July 1862, created colleges and universities by using the proceeds from federal land sales. Some of the colleges that were created due to this act are among the best in the US even today. The Morrill Act granted each state a tract of land to endow A&M colleges (Agricultural and Mechanical colleges). These schools were designed to give students in the lower classes an opportunity to receive higher education. They were also given the task of developing better farm equipment and better processes for future agricultural success.

Each of these schools was required to teach mechanical arts, agriculture, and military tactics. A good example of a famous A&M college today is Texas A&M, which has a well-known cadet program.

Before the Morrill Act was passed, higher education in the US was quite different. Universities often taught classical studies, which required the knowledge of dead languages, barring the working classes from attending. The Southerners in Congress often hailed from affluent families, and many of them wanted to keep the wealth in their own hands, so the act was only able to be passed once they seceded from the Union. When the act first passed, it only applied to those states that did not secede, but in time, it grew to include all the states in the Union.

The Pacific Railway Act

Since people were moving westward following the Homestead Act, it only seemed reasonable to build a transcontinental railroad. In July of 1862, President Lincoln signed the Pacific Railway Act, which aimed to link the East with the underdeveloped West.

Before secession, this was a hot topic along regional lines, as Northerners wanted the railroad to travel a northern route while the Southerners battled for a southern route. Following the departure of the Democrats, the Republican Congress devised a middle path that quickly passed both Houses. The railroad would start at Council Bluffs, Missouri, and end at Sacramento, California.

The construction of this transcontinental railroad was a godsend for Northern factories and workers. Thousands were able to get jobs, while the South was, for the most part, left out. This was probably not only due to the South seceding from the Union but also because building the railroad was an industrial job, and Southerners had minimal industrial experience. The railroad linked the uncharted West with established cities in the East, leaving behind the South, at least for now.

Financial Legislation

The next three pieces of legislation belong to the country's financial realm. They established standards and laws that we still follow today. However, each of these acts was a thorn in the South's side.

The Legal Tender Act

The first of these acts was the Legal Tender Act. It gave the federal government the power to print and use paper money to pay for the war. Until this act, it had been policy to only use gold and silver to pay for government actions. This would allow the use of paper money when the reserves of silver and gold were depleted. The bill aimed to finance the war without raising taxes, and it worked incredibly well. Even though the so-called "greenbacks" were not backed by silver or gold in similar amounts, businesses were still required by law to accept the greenbacks at face value. Due to its success, these paper notes paved the way for a national currency in the United States. The Union printed around 450 million dollars during the war.

The Internal Revenue Act

The North struggled to finance the war, and in 1861, the Revenue Act was passed. It was the first income tax ever levied on the public, placing more of the burden on the shoulders of the wealthy. However, before the first income tax was ever collected, the US government passed the second Revenue Act in 1862. This adjusted the income tax, separating the taxpayers into levels based on their incomes. It also established the predecessor for the Internal Revenue Service (IRS) and levied excise taxes on the people, which greatly affected lower-income Americans.

The National Bank Act

The National Bank Act, which was passed in 1863, was an attempt to create a federal bank. It delineated a plan to create a single federal currency and a system of national banks, which would counter the smaller, local banks. This act was particularly abhorrent to the South, as they emphasized states' rights and limited federal rule. They knew that national banks would be more tightly regulated by the government. This act improved the Union's financial situation, but it did not cure its financial ills.

The Southerners believed in a small federal government and strong state control. The agricultural and slavery-driven economy of the South did not lend itself to any strong central government or financial organization. This type of economy turned out to be a significant disadvantage in the war. The South could not build the same financial programs as the North, so it was not set up for success and growth after the war ended.

The Condition of the Union after the War

President Andrew Johnson faced the massive challenge of bringing the Confederate states back into the Union and integrating around four million freed slaves into society. The South was decimated with no currency and no workforce.

In 1861, 297 cities and towns in the Confederacy had a population of around 835,000. At some point during the war, any city or town with a population of over 681,000 had Union forces occupying them. Sherman's March to the Sea involved burning Atlanta to the ground and destroying Charleston, Richmond, and Columbia. Smaller towns suffered less damage, but they were still economically devastated.

On the plantations and farms, 40 percent of the mules, horses, and cattle were killed. In addition to the destruction of land and animals, there was also damage done to the farmers' machines and farming implements. The war destroyed the architecture and infrastructure of the South. Riverboats and railroads were in short supply due to the Southern policy of destroying them as they retreated. Even if they had crops and animals to sell, very little could be moved to market.

Most of the rest of the transportation system, including bridges, rail yards, rolling transportation stock, and repair shops, was also in disrepair. When the Union Army moved through the South, they destroyed anything they could.

Between the loss of human lives, physical destruction, and the overwhelming expense of the war, the South was in a poor state. The Confederacy had also run up a total debt of over 1.4 billion dollars. The Confederate dollar was worthless, and its banking system was failing. Bartering became the currency of the post-war South, as the economic system as a whole had to be rebuilt, this time without slave labor. Due to the war, many plantation owners had little money to pay for the labor of freed blacks. This situation led to the sharecropper economy. Former slaves became sharecroppers, living on the land and working it but paying the majority of their profits to the landowners. The economy changed from wealthy plantation owners to agricultural tenant farmers.

The end of the war also brought about a large migration to the North. Freed people moved to the urban areas in droves, taking any jobs they could find, mostly in the service industry or a sector that required unskilled labor. Black women largely engaged in domestic work and remained there for generations. They took care of white children, cleaned homes, took in laundry, or became cooks. Men worked in lumber mills, on the railroads, and in hotels.

Meanwhile, the white population in the South was decimated, as almost 25 percent of the young men were killed. These men were the breadwinners for their families, which meant many were driven into poverty. All of these factors locked the South into a multigenerational cycle of poverty, and these were the challenges that faced the Union government during the Reconstruction era.

The damage was not nearly as devastating in the North, although there had been a massive loss of life there as well. The North lost more people than the South, but the North's population was also far greater, even before the migration of the freed people. It is believed the North suffered over 828,000 (over 365,000 dead) casualties, while the South had around 864,000 (over 290,000 dead). This includes dead, wounded, captured, and missing.

At one point during the war, the Union was spending nearly one million dollars per week. Overall expenditures can only be estimated, but Claudia Goldin and Frank Lewis have made the best estimations to date in their report, "The Economic Cost of the American Civil War: Estimates and Implications," which was written in 1975. The following monetary costs were included:

For the North:

Government expenditures were around 2.3 billion dollars.

The loss of human capital was around 1.1 billion dollars.

Property loss was zero for the North.

For the South:

Government expenditures were around 1 billion dollars.

The loss of human capital was around 767 million dollars.

Property loss was 1.5 billion for the South.

In his last speech before he died, Lincoln discussed the possibility of giving freed blacks and those who had served in the military the right to vote. Four days later, Lincoln was assassinated. Lincoln had an idea of how he wanted the Reconstruction efforts to take shape. Instead, the role was suddenly thrust upon Andrew Johnson. Let's take a look at how Lincoln envisioned Reconstruction.

Chapter 2 – Lincoln's Vision

One of Lincoln's greatest visions actually occurred during the Civil War; this was the famous Emancipation Proclamation. The other piece of his vision that never came to fruition was something known as the Ten Percent Plan.

The Emancipation Proclamation

An incredible thing happened on September 22nd, 1862, in the United States of America. This had an impact on both the Union and the Confederacy, and it had long-reaching implications for the nation as a whole.

What was this incredible thing? On September 22nd, 1862, President Abraham Lincoln courageously issued an executive order. On January 1st, 1863, all slaves held in bondage in the Confederacy would forever be free. Even more critical were the phrases in this presidential proclamation that stated this freedom would be recognized and protected by the United States military.

The Emancipation Proclamation was something abolitionists had been dreaming of for decades. The Fugitive Slave Act of 1850 struck a severe blow to abolitionism, as it required runaway slaves to be returned to their owners even if they managed to cross into a state that no longer had slavery. When the Civil War broke out, Lincoln wanted this law gone, mainly because it implied the Confederacy was a separate nation that had to be respected.

The Dred Scott case of 1857 set black people back even more. Dred Scott was a slave whose owners took him from the slave-holding state of Missouri into Illinois, where slavery was illegal. Scott sued for his freedom, but the US Supreme Court ruled that the US Constitution did not include black people when they used the term "citizens." By June of 1862, both Congress and Lincoln were prepared to defy this Supreme Court decision. Lincoln had been worried about going against the Constitution and dismantling slavery during his presidential run, but he ultimately signed the legislation passed by Congress, outlawing slavery in all of the current Union states and any future states. This action confined slavery to the states where it already existed. Congress then passed the Confiscation Act of 1862 in July of the same year. This legislation set up a process for freeing slaves owned by convicted rebels or those abandoning the Union Army. Of course, these actions alienated the Confederate states even more and laid the groundwork for the Emancipation Proclamation.

Lincoln freed the slaves with the Emancipation Proclamation; well, he at least freed the slaves in the Confederate States of America. Those slaves who lived in the border states were still stuck in the same position as before. These states were Maryland, Kentucky, Delaware, Missouri, and West Virginia. It was thought that if the slaves were freed in these states, the people might turn to the Confederacy, putting the North in a more precarious position. However, of the four million slaves in the nation, more than three and a half million slaves were granted their freedom under this federal law. Eventually, either federal or state actions freed the slaves in the border states as well.

From this point onward, any slave who found their way across Union lines or living in an area liberated by Union soldiers was permanently and immediately free. When the North won the war, all slaves everywhere were freed with the passage of the Thirteenth Amendment, which was ratified in December of 1865.

The Republican drive to free the slaves during the Civil War was egged on by the Northern press. In one notable incident, the *New-York Tribune* ran an editorial by Horace Greeley, who called for the end to slavery in all the states. Greeley stated that slavery would continue to present a danger to the Union even after the war ended. In response, Lincoln maintained that his only duty was to save the Union, even if that meant slavery still existed. Despite saying this publicly, Lincoln was morally opposed to slavery and desired to free the people held in bondage. Lincoln's response was posited to soften any white opposition in the North who didn't support the idea of abolition by tying it to the Union's survival.

In fact, Lincoln had already drafted a preliminary proclamation before he even addressed Greeley's concerns. US historian Todd Brewster believes that Lincoln sought to end slavery but realized he needed to frame it in a way that would sit well with the American public. By using a war-related proclamation to free the slaves in the rebel states, Lincoln and his attorney general believed they could remain free, regardless of the decision in the Dred Scott case.

Even though the Emancipation Proclamation is remembered best for doing the right and moral thing by setting the slaves in the Confederacy free, it can also be seen as a military move, as the Emancipation Proclamation allowed freed slaves to join the Union Army, giving the North an additional source of manpower. However, they often weren't given combat roles and were instead given hard, dirty tasks, like digging trenches. They were not paid as much as white soldiers, and they were often given poorer equipment. Despite this, black people joined the army in droves, as they were fighting for something they held dear, and it is believed that blacks made up 10 percent of the Union Army. Black people also helped to feed soldiers and repaired anything from railroads to uniforms. In addition to that, they also worked in many areas of the Northern economy.

When Lincoln issued the Emancipation Proclamation, he understood that freeing all the slaves would require a constitutional amendment since the proclamation only dealt with those states in the Confederacy. Lincoln worked on a series of amendments to make the process of abolition smoother, but none of them passed. By the time January 1ˢᵗ, 1863, rolled around, the Emancipation Proclamation was in effect, forever changing history in the United States. Although those in the North were hopeful for a brighter future, there was still a lot of resentment in both halves of the country.

In May 1863, the Confederacy passed their own legislation, calling for "full and ample retaliation" against the Union. They were worried that the sight of black men in uniform would stir something inside the slaves, something that would inspire them to throw off their chains and fight back. Before this legislation was passed, members of the Confederate Congress even suggested killing all captured Union soldiers, whether they were black or white. In the end, it was decided that black soldiers fighting for the Union who were captured by the Confederacy would be treated as runaway slaves. The Confederacy even increased the price for a slave after the Emancipation Proclamation because they believed there would be even more support for slavery in the South.

Part of Lincoln's plan for the Reconstruction included a requirement for every Southern state to abolish slavery by state law. Without this law in place, the state could not reenter the Union. His post-war plan also included the passage of the Thirteenth Amendment, which was ultimately passed and ended slavery in the United States.

The Emancipation Proclamation and the Gettysburg Address (the speech he gave at the dedication of the Soldiers' National Cemetery) are perhaps the most memorable moments of Lincoln's presidential career.

The Ten Percent Plan

The Emancipation Proclamation radically changed what was at stake in the war. If the Union won under these conditions, it would create a major social revolution in the Southern states once they returned to the fold. In light of this, Lincoln spent most of his time considering how to reunite the rebel states with the Union. How could Reconstruction bring the Union closer together rather than allowing the bitterness to divide it more?

Once Lincoln saw that the Union was moving toward total victory, he turned his attention to this challenge. Since Lincoln believed the South never "legally" seceded, he wanted the Reconstruction to be forgiving and not punitive. It was along these lines that he issued the Proclamation of Amnesty and Reconstruction in early December 1863.

This proclamation was built on the foundation of the Emancipation Proclamation, and it offered the rebel states a conciliatory way to rejoin the Union. Lincoln had no desire to punish the rebel states; after all, his goal from the beginning of the war was focused on saving the *entire* Union.

There were three major points in this proclamation.

> • A full pardon would be granted to everyone involved in the rebellion, including the restoration of their property. The only exception was the top-level Confederate Army officers and the top-level civilian officials of the Confederate government. Lincoln promised the rejoining Southerners that he would protect their private property except for their slaves.

- When ten percent of all eligible voters in the Confederate States of America sworn allegiance to the United States, a new state government could be formed.
- The states that participated in the first two steps were then to design and enact plans for integrating the freed slaves into the community without compromising their liberties.

In time, this proclamation became better known as the Ten Percent Plan. It was a plan that the South could have swallowed without a lot of rancor and bitterness, and it was a much more charitable plan than most people on both sides had expected. Perhaps it was too generous.

Some in Congress bowed to Lincoln's power and prestige, saying they believed the Ten Percent Plan would end the war and reunite the nation quickly. Lincoln believed this as well, for he feared the longer the war went on, the lower the chance of reuniting the Union. In his mind, the proclamation was actually an enticement for the South to surrender. He was also worried about the upcoming election in 1864; if the Democrats regained control, all of his work would be undone.

Lincoln's vision included a self-reconstruction by the reunited states. In other words, the federal government would not have a significant role or offer major assistance in their post-Civil War efforts. Three states rejoined the Union by 1864: Louisiana, Tennessee, and Arkansas. Louisiana promised its citizens many benefits for rejoining the Union peacefully. These benefits included public works projects, public schools for all without cost, and improvements to labor systems. Louisiana also abolished slavery, although it did not give the right to vote to the freed slaves.

However, not all in Congress agreed with this plan. The Radical Republicans wanted more punitive measures taken against the South, including the disbandment of the planter aristocracy. The Radical Republicans held the minority, but they managed to introduce a bill to the floor that held some support, which will be covered in the next chapter.

Chapter 3 – The Wade-Davis Bill and the Radical Republicans

During the Civil War, there were two opposing camps within the Republican Party. On one side, there was Abraham Lincoln and the moderates, and on the other side were the Radical Republicans. For Lincoln and the moderates, it was vital to handle Reconstruction as quickly as possible and get the Union reunited. However, the Radical Republicans wanted to see slavery completely and immediately destroyed, no matter the cost.

The Republican Party was split into moderates and Radicals from around 1854 until 1877, the year Reconstruction ended. Most Radical Republicans were inspired by religious or moral institutions that saw slavery as evil. Many of them were Christians and/or were a part of the abolitionist movements in the US. The more extreme Christians believed that the Civil War was a punishment from God for the sin of slavery.

Some of the most prominent Radical Republicans included William H. Seward, the US secretary of state under Lincoln and Johnson; Thaddeus Stevens, a US congressman from Pennsylvania; and Horace Greeley, a newspaper editor. There were many other influential people who sided with the Radicals, such as Ulysses S. Grant, Edwin Stanton, John A. Logan, and Benjamin Butler.

Thaddeus Stevens was perhaps the most notable leader of the Radical Republicans. Stevens had been an ardent abolitionist for many years. Before entering Congress, Stevens was a Pennsylvania lawyer with many freedom-seeking clients. Once in Congress, he chaired the House Ways and Means Committee and was one of the House's most influential members. During the war, Stevens constantly prodded Lincoln on the issue of freeing the slaves. He did not believe the Confederate states should reenter the Union without meeting rigid requirements. In fact, Stevens viewed the seceded states as conquered provinces.

While Stevens piloted the House, Charles Sumner led the Radical Republicans in the Senate. Sumner had no qualms in making his stance known, and he once paid the price for it. In an anti-slavery speech he gave in 1856, Sumner called a South Carolina senator a "pimp for slavery," and his first cousin, Preston Brooks, a congressman from South Carolina, beat Sumner so badly with his cane that he almost died. Stevens's and Sumner's commitment and passion made the Radical Republicans a powerful force during and after the war. Even Vice President Andrew Johnson sided with the Radicals on some issues.

Lincoln attempted to bring the Radicals, the moderates, conservatives, and the loyal "war" Democrats into a coalition. Unfortunately, this effort failed. It was not until 1872 that a group called the Liberal Republicans challenged the Radicals. These Republicans advocated for a return to classic republicanism, and even though they garnered Democrat support, their efforts to win the presidency failed.

The power of the Radical Republicans can also be seen in the twenty-one pieces of legislation that Johnson vetoed during his presidency. Out of these twenty-one vetoes, Congress overrode fifteen of them. The Radical Republicans' work also led to ten Republican governments forming in the previous Confederate states.

In 1866, the Radical Republicans took control of Congress due to their opposition to President Johnson's Reconstruction policies. Plenty of violence had resulted from these policies, and it was more than enough for Northern voters to consider voting for a more radical faction. The Memphis riots and the New Orleans riots of 1866 are a few examples of the violence that took place.

When Lincoln proposed the Ten Percent Plan back in 1863, both moderate Republicans and proslavery Democrats, in addition to the Radical Republicans, opposed his Reconstruction plans. In opposition to the Ten Percent Plan, the Radical Republicans passed their own Reconstruction plan, which is known as the Wade-Davis Bill. Lincoln pocket-vetoed their plan in 1864 (meaning he took no action to enact the bill) because it was too harsh.

The Wade-Davis Bill

The Wade-Davis Bill was rather extreme. The Radical Republicans who passed it wanted 50 percent of the seceded state's voters to take a loyalty oath before the state could be readmitted to the Union. Once this happened, then a state convention could be called to create a new state constitution. Every voter had to swear loyalty to the Union if he wanted to vote. Any state reentering the Union had to ban slavery and guarantee protections for the freed people. Although Republicans insisted the bill should include black men's right to vote, the final version did not include that wording. It was all irrelevant in the end anyway due to Lincoln's displeasure with the bill.

Lincoln thought this plan would only prolong the war he was trying to end, which was why he chose not to sign the bill before Congress recessed that year. This pocket veto effectively killed the bill.

Many Radical Republicans wanted equal rights for blacks, including the right to vote. It seems that before Lincoln was assassinated by John Wilkes Booth, he was also leaning in that direction. In his last speech, which he gave on April 11th, 1865, four days before his death, Lincoln hinted that blacks who served in the military should have the right to vote.

Lincoln's vision for the country's reunification never had a chance to be fully put in place, as he died before the war ended. After Lincoln was assassinated, Vice President Andrew Johnson, a Democrat, succeeded to the presidency. Without Lincoln, Congress dissolved into bitter arguments about the Reconstruction with President Johnson.

Chapter 4 – The Thirteenth Amendment

The Thirteenth Amendment

It is not an easy process to amend the Constitution of the United States. It takes a lot of work, a lot of patience, and usually several years. This endeavor is not undertaken lightly, but it seems most politicians were ready for a change in 1865 when the Thirteenth Amendment became an official part of the Constitution.

Lincoln had used his executive powers as commander-in-chief to issue the Emancipation Proclamation. However, there was some concern that once the war was over, the proclamation would have no teeth. A constitutional amendment freeing the slaves was the only way to be sure abolitionism was the law of the land.

As the war winded down, Congress began to look at how to reunite all the states and how the nation could live in harmony afterward. The radical anti-slavery coalitions started to push for a constitutional amendment to make slavery illegal permanently in the country. A bill was introduced to Congress on December 14th, 1863, to create such an amendment. Representatives James Michell Ashley from Ohio and James F. Wilson from Iowa presented the bill to the House of Representatives. In January of 1864, the Senate received its version through a joint resolution submitted by John B. Henderson of Missouri. These different proposals all went to the Senate Judiciary Committee to have their differences resolved. However, the Radical Republicans were not happy with any of these versions. Charles Sumner presented the Senate with their version on February 8th, 1864.

The Radical Republicans' amendment was simple and straightforward. It stated, "All persons are equal before the law, so that no person can hold another as a slave; and the Congress shall have power to make all laws necessary and proper to carry this declaration into effect everywhere in the United States."

Sumner tried to avoid the Judiciary Committee for consideration of his amendment, as he wanted his own committee to take a look at it, but the Senate sent it there anyway. The Senate Judiciary Committee did not take this version into consideration as they did with the others. Instead, they submitted a version to the Senate based on Wilson's, Ashley's, and Henderson's works.

The Thirteenth Amendment is short and direct. It contains two sections, which you can read below:

Section 1

"Neither slavery nor involuntary servitude, except as a punishment for crime whereof the party shall have been duly convicted, shall exist within the United States, or any place subject to their jurisdiction."

Section 2

"The Congress shall have power to enforce this article by appropriate legislation."

The Senate Judiciary Committee mainly based their draft on Henderson's version, but they did not agree with his stipulation that a constitutional amendment could only be adopted by a majority vote in the House and Senate and ratification by two-thirds of the state legislatures. The rule at the time was two-thirds of each House of Congress and three-fourths of the states.

At the Senate vote on April 8th, 1864, the measure passed. The House had more trouble agreeing. The Democrats, who opposed the amendment, relied on the arguments of states' rights and federalism. Some believed the amendment signaled revolution as opposed to just being a constitutional amendment. These Democrats thought the amendment went against the spirit of the Constitution, while others argued that it would lead to full citizenship for black people. On the other side, Republicans argued that slavery was immoral and uncivilized. They believed that white people were injured by slavery as well. After all, employment rates in the slave states were much lower than in the North due to slave labor. Soon, many Northern Democrats came to support the amendment.

Following his re-election, Lincoln threw his administration's power behind the amendment. He made it the top priority of his second term. Members of his administration plied Democrats with promises of campaign contributions or positions in the government. When the House appeared to be only a handful of votes from passing the second vote, Lincoln went all out to secure its passage. The amendment passed the House on January 31st, 1865.

On February 1st, 1865, the amendment was sent to the states to be ratified. At that time, there were thirty-six states in the Union, including those states that had seceded. Out of that number, twenty-seven states would have to ratify the amendment for it to become the law of the land. In less than thirty days, eighteen states had already ratified it. Most of the Northern states ratified the amendment very quickly, as did most of the loyal border states. However, they didn't pass it quickly enough for Lincoln to see the nation freed. The final approval of the amendment was due to the Johnson administration's work in currying the favor of North Carolina, Alabama, and Georgia. By gaining their accession, the amendment had the required number of twenty-seven states, and the amendment became a part of the United States Constitution before the end of the year.

The Effectiveness of the Thirteenth Amendment

Once the amendment was ratified, celebration broke out, especially among the Radical Republicans and the black population. There were both immediate and long-term ramifications of this action. To review some of the most significant impacts:

- The system of chattel slavery that existed before the war was made illegal.

- In Kentucky, between 65,000 and 100,000 slaves were freed immediately.

- In Delaware, around 900 individuals immediately became freed people.

- The Fugitive Slave Clause was nullified, as was the Three-Fifths Compromise. The Three-Fifths Compromise was added to the US Constitution in 1787, and it gave a boost to the Southern states, which were not as populous as the North. According to the compromise, every three out of five slaves would be counted as people. With the passage of the Thirteenth Amendment, former slaves would all count for demographic reasons and to increase Congress's apportionment in the South.

- Millions of slaves were freed, but they had no way of supporting themselves or their families. They had no land and no opportunities except to stay on the plantations and work for low wages. However, even though they were earning money now, they were no longer sheltered and fed by the plantation owners.

- All the slaves had been freed without appropriate protections or legal status. Some historians believe they were treated even worse than they had been as slaves, as there were no protections in place.

- Laws were passed in the South to criminalize as many blacks as possible. These were called the Black Codes.

- The Thirteenth Amendment allowed for the punishment of forced labor for those convicted of a crime. The Northwest Ordinance of 1787 included the same type of wording, as Congress had simply lifted it and added it to the amendment. There was no consideration of the ramifications of this clause. This clause is still a part of the amendment, although current legislators are attempting to change it.

The Thirteenth Amendment certainly ended chattel slavery. However, it didn't necessarily make the lives of freed people much easier. Slavery could still be used as a punishment for crime, and laws, known as the Black Codes, were designed to essentially trap black people into committing crimes. For instance, blacks could be sentenced to forced labor for selling cotton after sunset or not contracting with a white farmer; if they refused to sign the contract, they would be considered vagrants. Freed people were subjected to violence, white supremacy, and the inconsistent enforcement of laws. Of course, most of this took place in the South, but the North was not blameless.

This clause resulted in many ex-slaves being imprisoned on old plantations and being subjected to involuntary labor. The prisoners saw the guards at these sites as just another overseer. The Virginia Supreme Court even justified this treatment in 1871. In this ruling, the court declared the prisoners to be slaves of the state.

So, regardless of the designers' intentions, this amendment did not confer any civil rights on the black population, and they faced an uphill battle. The Reconstruction policies should have helped alleviate the problem, but as you will discover in the following pages, they didn't go far enough.

Judicial Reviews of the Thirteenth Amendment

The Thirteenth Amendment brought a lot of change to the nation, and as a result, it was questioned time and time again or used to support a ruling. The first time a high-level court was asked to look at the Thirteenth Amendment was in 1866. Here is a brief overview of some of the cases.

1866 – *United States v. Rhodes* concerned black people's ability to get redress in the federal courts. In this case, Kentucky had a law that did not allow blacks to testify against whites. The lawsuit specifically involved a black woman who was robbed by a white man. Since the woman was unable to testify against the man, it prevented her from attaining justice.

The Kentucky Supreme Court ruled that the woman could not appeal to the federal courts for redress. However, a Supreme Court justice overruled the Kentucky decision based on the Civil Rights Act of 1866, which set the foundation for black citizenship in the US.

1872 – In *Blyew v. United States*, two white men were visiting the cabin of a black family. John Blyew became angry and hit one of the sons on the head with an ax twice. The two men then killed his parents and grandmother. They also seriously wounded two of the younger children.

The Supreme Court ruled that the children didn't have a case because only living people could take advantage of the Civil Rights Act. In other words, this meant the Thirteenth Amendment did not provide any relief in murder cases. Not all the justices agreed with this ruling, saying that the Thirteenth Amendment needed to be interpreted in a way that would give black people some standing in society. However, they were in the minority. This case set a precedent and led to the Thirteenth Amendment's loss of power.

1896 – The attorneys in the case of *Plessy v. Ferguson* used the Thirteenth Amendment to argue against racial segregation. They argued that because of segregation, there were "observances of a servile character coincident with the incidents of slavery," which was in violation of the Thirteenth Amendment. The lawyers argued that the "distinction between race and caste" violated the Constitution. Unfortunately, the Supreme Court didn't agree, saying that it could not eliminate social legalities and distinctions that were based on color. It was up to the state to decide which laws to pass and if they were reasonable enough. This was the famous "separate but equal" decision.

1906 – In *Hodges v. United States*, the Supreme Court again used the Thirteenth Amendment, this time to prevent justice for those who conspired to commit violence. A group of white men used violent means to prevent a group of black men from working. The white men were convicted in Kentucky of a conspiracy to deprive citizens of their liberty. However, the US Supreme Court ruled that violent assault or aggression did not "reduce the individual to a condition of slavery." Therefore, they declared the Kentucky ruling to be unconstitutional.

1911 – In *Bailey v. Alabama*, the Supreme Court ruled that the Thirteenth Amendment covered more than just chattel slavery. The court ruled that "The plain intention [of the amendment] was to abolish slavery of whatever name and form and all its badges and incidents; to render impossible any state of bondage; to make labor free, by prohibiting that control by which the personal service of one man is disposed of or coerced for another's benefit, which is the essence of involuntary servitude."

1968 – *Jones v. Alfred H. Mayer Co.* is an interesting example of how far the interpretation of the Thirteenth Amendment had stretched by the 20th century. The Jones family sued the Alfred H. Mayer real estate company for not selling them a home. The Supreme Court ruled that Congress may act "to prevent private actors from imposing badges and incidents of servitude." Congress had the authority under the Thirteenth Amendment to decide what those "badges and incidents of servitude" were. The Supreme Court also upheld the Civil Rights Act of 1866, saying that it prohibited private and state-backed discrimination.

There were many other cases that involved the Thirteenth Amendment. Some of the more recent ones include when the US Supreme Court ruled that the military draft did not equate to involuntary servitude during the Vietnam War or when the US Court of Appeals ruled that schools imposing community service as a condition of high school graduation did not engage in involuntary servitude.

Although the Thirteenth Amendment still has ramifications for today's society, back in the 1860s, people feared what the effects of the amendment might mean for the nation. President Andrew Johnson fully approved of the Thirteenth Amendment, but he tried to placate some of those fears, especially for those living in the South, during his Reconstruction efforts.

Chapter 5 – Presidential Reconstruction

Most historians believe that if Lincoln had lived, the Reconstruction would have been drastically different. For one, there would have been a substantial federal role in overseeing the entire Reconstruction era. Andrew Johnson did not think the federal government should play a major role in this at all. But Johnson was a Democrat, and having more power in the federal government instead of the states' hands went against their beliefs.

Following the passage of the Thirteenth Amendment, Congress was in recess. President Andrew Johnson decided this was a good time for him to design his own Reconstruction plan. This period is known as the "Presidential Reconstruction." During this time, President Johnson oversaw the new Southern governments and the states' political conventions as they reentered the Union. Johnson chose the delegates to these conventions based on their loyalty to him.

Johnson would not demand much from the Confederate states rejoining the Union. Three major issues faced each state in their conventions to become a part of the nation again. These issues were the secession, the abolition of slavery, and resolving the war debt. Once the states reunited with the Union, Johnson believed the

Southern states should then take control of their own government and Reconstruction efforts.

The first conventions, which were held in 1865, took place in North Carolina, Alabama, South Carolina, Florida, Mississippi, and Georgia. Johnson wanted the Thirteenth Amendment ratified by all the Southern states before Congress reconvened that December. He knew he would be in a fight over the Reconstruction efforts with the Radical Republicans, and he wanted the leverage the South could bring him. If he ratified the Thirteenth Amendment, freeing the slaves in the process, Johnson would be able to point to the willingness of the Southern states to change and embrace a new way of life. By doing this, Johnson would show the American public that it would be wrong to let the Southern states stay out of the Union while also demonstrating the South's ability to make the right decisions on their own, without major interference from the federal government.

However, to do this, Johnson had to negotiate with the Southern states, offering them a vision of how they could enact the amendment. Johnson certainly wanted freed people to enjoy some rights, but he went so far as to promise Southern governors that they would control how they gave out rights to the freed slaves. This would have allowed the white supremacists in the South to have a large role in how the Reconstruction proceeded. In time, they made it incredibly difficult for blacks to hold office or even vote. They also demanded that the freed slaves return any land that the federal government had granted them under the "forty acres and a mule" order. This land went back to the former slave owners, leaving the blacks with no land and no money.

The promise of "forty acres and a mule" had been made by Union General William Tecumseh Sherman. General Sherman had land in Florida, Georgia, and South Carolina reserved for the resettlement of the freed slaves. If a freed slave took an oath of loyalty to the Union, they were eligible to settle on and lease up to forty acres of land. He also planned for there to be an option to purchase the land in a few years. Sadly, this promise was an empty one due to President Johnson's administration. Although some black people were able to take advantage of it, it never happened in the way that Sherman had planned.

Even though Johnson did his best to placate the South over the Thirteenth Amendment, the wording of it did not please all the Southern politicians. The Southern governments were afraid the North would use the enforcement clause (the one that states Congress has the power to pass legislation to support the amendment) to impose blacks suffrage everywhere in the Union. Several Southern states ratified the amendment with stipulations that Congress could not legislate policy that went against the Constitution in regards to the former slaves.

President Johnson's basic attitude was one of laissez-faire and strong state governments. Unlike the Radical Republicans, he favored states' rights and a less powerful central government. He believed the federal government had no business interfering in the economy and social life of the states, which led him to oppose legislation that impacted the economy in any way.

In an attempt to keep the Radical Republicans from challenging his plans, Johnson declared the end of Reconstruction before Congress even reconvened in 1865. Congress was furious, and when the members reconvened, they passed a series of bills, some of which Johnson vetoed. He objected to reorganizing the economy of the South or dismantling the plantation system, and he did not hold many strong beliefs in regards to protecting the civil rights of the freed slaves. While he expected the blacks to have some rights, Johnson did not believe that blacks should have the same rights as the white population, routinely calling black people inferior.

Needless to say, Johnson's legacy is a bit mixed. Some scholars believe he tried his best to carry out Lincoln's vision, even though he didn't agree with all of his policies. He refused to bend to Congress's whim, a Congress that consistently voted against his vetoes, and he worked on a plan that adhered strictly to the Constitution. This plan ultimately failed, and Congress essentially took the reins from him. But even Johnson's supporters realize that he wasn't a strong leader. He certainly was not the best person to oversee the Reconstruction. He also wasn't as committed to the Reconstruction efforts as other leaders, such as Lincoln, would have been, and he wasn't a man that compromised, which affected the freed slaves most of all, as they did not have a good footing in society.

Chapter 6 – The Civil Rights Act of 1866

The Joint Committee on Reconstruction, 1865

When the Radical Republicans came back into session in December of 1865, they found that President Johnson had conducted and completed his Reconstruction plan. They also discovered that he had pardoned many influential and high-ranking Southerners and let them keep their lands. In their eyes, this Reconstruction was too soft on the South. The Radicals knew Johnson's Reconstruction efforts were even worse than what Lincoln had planned.

The Radical Republicans knew they had to do something. Not only were they angered by Johnson's actions, but they also felt disrespected. The Republicans were greatly concerned that Johnson's Reconstruction held no security for the freed slaves and that instead of helping those who had just escaped bondage, the president chose to appease Southern plantation owners who had left the Union.

To combat these actions, Congress established the Joint Committee on Reconstruction in late 1865 to establish its own plan. This coalition, which included three Democrats, gave the Radicals enough power to put the Reconstruction in the hands of Congress. This led to veto after veto from Johnson, although Congress was able to override most of them. Johnson's attempt to create a coalition of moderates failed to overcome the power of the Radicals, who were able to legislate their plan for Reconstruction.

This plan began with the Civil Rights Act of 1866.

In 1865 and 1866, many of the former Confederate states passed legislation known as the Black Codes. These will be discussed in more depth later on, but for now, it is important to understand that these codes were meant to keep freed slaves from going where or doing what they wanted. Their goal was to keep the freed people as a source of labor in the South.

The Black Codes were the forerunners of the infamous Jim Crow laws, and they enraged the Radical Republicans and the abolitionists of the North. Congress's first response was to refuse to allow any senator or congress member from the South to be seated in the new Congress. While they were unable to keep Southern representatives out of the government, the Radical Republicans did have an overwhelming majority in both Houses of Congress by 1866. In the first half of 1866, the Republicans got to work and passed two major pieces of legislation. These were the Civil Rights Act of 1866 and the Freedmen's Bureau Act.

The Civil Rights Act of 1866

As Southern states pushed the limits with the Black Codes, Radical Republicans needed a way to push back. That way was the Civil Rights Act of 1866.

In general, the law defined citizenship and affirmed that all citizens were equal under the law. This act aimed to protect the rights and citizenship of those who had African descent and were born in the United States.

By utilizing the power Congress had given itself in the Thirteenth Amendment, Senator Lyman Trumbull authored a bill that would actually benefit black people. Trumbull is also notable for his work on the Thirteenth Amendment. Congress passed the act on April 9th,

1886, but it was not ratified until 1870. To begin with, Johnson vetoed the act two separate times, once in 1865 and again in 1866. There was a general belief among politicians (not just Johnson) that Congress could not give itself the power to define citizenship. There needed to be a constitutional amendment for that. However, there was a two-thirds majority in both the House and Senate that supported the act, and they easily overrode the presidential veto the second time around.

The Civil Rights Act of 1866 is quite long, but we will take a closer look at the most important parts.

Section One of the Civil Rights Act

This is the most important part of the bill, as it bestows upon all people born in the United States, besides the Native Americans, the right to citizenship. It grants these citizens "of every race and color, without regard to any previous condition of slavery or involuntary servitude, except as a punishment for a crime whereof the party shall have been duly convicted" the "same right in every State and Territory to make and enforce contracts, to sue, be parties, give evidence, and to the full and equal benefit of all laws and proceedings for the security of persons and property as is enjoyed by white citizens, and shall be subject to like punishment, pains, penalties, taxes, licenses, and exactions of every kind, and to no other."

Just this opening section was anathema to the members of the former Confederate States of America, as black people who had been born into slavery in the United States had automatic citizenship. Given that President Johnson's sympathies lay with the South, this first section alone gave him enough ammunition to veto the bill. What Southerner would agree that former slaves and freemen had the right to enter into contracts and sue anyone in court? What Southerner would agree that former slaves and freemen could testify in court or buy, sell, or inherit property? What former Confederate would concur that these former slaves and freemen should enjoy the same laws as they did? These were the kind of ideas and laws that had started the Civil War in the first place. Johnson wanted to reunite the

Union without upsetting the South more than they already were. On top of that, this bill certainly did not fall in line with Johnson's Reconstruction plans.

You might have noticed that the Civil Rights Act did not extend to Native Americans. In actuality, it extended to those Native Americans who paid federal taxes, but there were very few of them. Most Native Americans at this time either lived on reservations or in unsettled territories. Since they did not pay federal taxes and were subject to their own reservation governments, the US government did not include them in census counts. In other words, they had no voice in Congress, so no one fought for their rights on the bigger stage of US politics. Native Americans became US citizens in 1924, but like African Americans, they had to jump through many hurdles before their voice could finally be heard, a struggle that is still ongoing today.

Section Two

This section didn't sit any better with the Southerners. The Civil Rights Act went on to state that anyone who went against this act—in other words, anyone who sought to curtail the liberties of another person as stated in the above section, regardless of their skin color— "shall be deemed guilty of a misdemeanor, and, on conviction shall be punished by fine not exceeding one thousand dollars, or imprisonment not exceeding one year, or both, in the discretion of the court."

Not only were the Northern Republicans in Congress saying that ex-slaves had the same rights as white Southerners, but they were also saying whites could go to jail if they didn't honor those rights. If you had been a son of the Confederacy, it would have only taken one quick read of this legislation to send you into a boiling rage. And we're not even halfway through the act.

Section Three

This is a rather lengthy section, but it really comes down to these words. "The jurisdiction in civil and criminal matters hereby conferred on the district and circuit courts of the United States shall be exercised and enforced in conformity with the laws of the United States, so far as such laws are suitable to carry the same into effect."

In other words, if a person of color cannot get a fair trial in the state courts, the federal district and circuit courts will have jurisdiction.

Section Four

This section talked about what would happen if someone violated this act. It states that "the district attorneys, marshals, and deputy marshals of the United States...and every other officer who may be specially empowered by the President of the United States, shall be, and they are hereby, specially authorized and required...to institute proceedings against all and every person who shall violate the provisions of this act and cause him or them to be arrested and imprisoned, or bailed, as the case may be, for trial before such court of the United States."

Highlights of the Other Sections

There were ten sections in all. While the first four are the most pertinent to the discussion of Reconstruction, there are notable parts in the other sections. For instance, section five gives the United States military the power to enforce the non-slavery clause. Section eight provides the president with the right to have the military take action if he has "reason to believe that offences have been or are likely to be committed against the provisions of this act." Finally, the act ends with the US Supreme Court having the final say over any issues arising from this act.

That is a lot to take in, but the bottom line is that it was good for those freed by the Thirteenth Amendment. However, the former Confederates, in addition to other Southerners as well as people in the North, didn't see the Civil Rights Act in such a positive light. The question was raised as to whether Congress had the constitutional authority to enact this law, and as a result of these discussions, it was not even ratified until after the Fourteenth Amendment, which defined US citizenship, was passed.

Truthfully, the act seems more impactful than it actually turned out to be. Under constant pressure from Democrats, a significant part of the act was deleted. This had stated, "there shall be no discrimination in civil rights or immunities among the inhabitants of any State or Territory of the United States on account of race, color, or previous condition of servitude." Congress could not lay out what they meant by "civil rights," and even Republicans were worried that the courts might interpret the term too broadly. It is also important to note that the Civil Rights Act of 1866 did not grant black men the right to vote.

The act contained much of the same language as the Fourteenth Amendment, including equality before the law. The same type of language can also be found in the Second Freedmen's Bureau Act of 1866. With all this repetition, it was evident where Congress, which was led by the Republicans, stood on slavery and civil rights for blacks.

Some sections of this law are still enforceable today, particularly the section granting every citizen the right to enter into contracts, to sue, to testify against another in court, and the security of a person's property.

It was not until the 20th century that the Supreme Court validated Trumbull's contention that the Thirteenth Amendment gave Congress the right to legislate on these matters. In fact, it was due to the question of how much authority Congress had that the Fourteenth Amendment was drawn up. This amendment enshrined the major provisions of the Civil Rights Act of 1866 so that no future Congress could change them.

But how did the act fare in the face of Southern defiance? It was not as successful as the Radical Republicans hoped it would be. The activities of the Ku Klux Klan negatively affected its implementation. Discrimination in housing and employment was effectively illegal according to this legislation, but that was not the reality. These issues were still being litigated in the 20th century.

Freedmen's Bureau

A vital part of the Radical Republicans' Reconstruction plan was the Freedmen's Bureau, which was created by Congress in 1865. This organization's goal was to assist former slaves through the Reconstruction era. The Freedmen's Bureau was designed to establish schools, distribute confiscated property, and provide food and supplies.

Lincoln was around when the Freedmen's Bureau Bill was passed, although he died a little over a month later. Since it was created during the war, the Freedmen's Bureau operated under the auspices of the United States Department of War. In the beginning, most of the workers at the Bureau were Union soldiers. During this time, Congress did not allocate funds or hire knowledgeable personnel to make the Freedmen's Bureau effective.

As one might expect, Southerners and ex-Confederates did not welcome the Bureau. Southerners who had lost land during the war fully expected to get it back. This was especially true because Lincoln and Johnson allowed high-level Confederate officials to keep their land. The more affluent people in the South were not intimidated by the Bureau and thwarted its effectiveness. It also didn't help that the Bureau's staff were poor soldiers who often ignored the Southern abuse of former slaves for a small payoff. The Bureau also faced strong opposition from President Johnson. Johnson believed that the federal government should not play a role in protecting the former slaves or interfering with the states' judicial systems.

Despite these issues, the Freedmen's Bureau still managed to do some good. It helped to resettle thousands of war refugees and built schools. By the end of 1865, more than 90,000 former slaves were enrolled in public schools.

Congress introduced and passed a new Freedmen's Bureau bill in 1866, adding special federal courts that could overrule the Southern state courts. However, President Johnson vetoed this bill. Congress worked hard on attaining a new bill that would please everyone, introducing a new one later that year. But yet again, Johnson vetoed it. This time around, Congress was able to agree, and they overrode the veto, which greatly displeased the president. In 1868, Congress tried to extend the Freedmen's Bureau, but they decided not to go ahead with the vote. Four years later, the Freedmen's Bureau closed.

In the seven years the Bureau was in operation, it had impressive success, even though it failed to accomplish all it had intended. The Freedmen's Bureau was set up into districts across the rebel states. Bureau personnel were spread out across the South, and usually, they were the only federal representatives in the area. They faced harassment, threats, violence, and ridicule.

The Bureau provided food for millions (including poor whites, although there was more of an emphasis on assisting the freed slaves), built schools and hospitals, and negotiated labor contracts for blacks. They also helped blacks find their family members from whom they had been separated.

Perhaps the Freedmen's Bureau's most significant accomplishment was establishing schools and universities. Before the Bureau, the South had no education system in place for blacks, and it is unlikely they would have created a state-sponsored education for the freed slaves, at least right away. Howard University owes its existence to the Bureau. The Freedmen's Bureau was also instrumental in establishing Hampton University in Virginia and Fisk University in Tennessee.

However, there were many shortcomings, and much of it had to do with the state of the South after the war. Since much of the infrastructure had been destroyed, the Bureau had to start from scratch. Racism was still prevalent, with white Southern doctors refusing to treat black people, which led to the spread of disease. In addition to this, members of the Bureau were regularly harassed and blocked from assisting where they were needed.

In March 1872, the commissioner of the Bureau was asked to head West to deal with the Native Americans. While he was gone, the Bureau steadily went under. The North was no longer invested in keeping the Bureau afloat. The South was still violent toward the Bureau's members, and it didn't seem to be getting any better as the years went by. In addition, by 1871, the South had formed constitutions that established universal public education, showing some progress when it came to equal rights. When the commissioner returned from the West that November, he found that the Bureau no longer existed.

Black Codes

Throughout the Reconstruction era, the South established something known as the Black Codes. These were the forerunners of the Jim Crow laws and were backed by a young Ku Klux Klan.

According to Southern politicians, the Black Codes were supposed to help revitalize the Southern economy. To be fair, the Southern economy was in dire straits. The war had done a lot of damage, and in addition to that, the slave labor force that the cotton and tobacco plantations had depended on had suddenly disappeared. As a result, the Black Codes were put in place so the blacks could still be used as a dependable labor force. However, many in the South saw this as the freed slaves' rightful place—a source of labor and nothing more. Southerners saw blacks who were not working as vagrants, which was punishable by the Black Codes. Freed people no longer wanted to work back-breaking hours; they wanted time to rest and enjoy themselves too, but many whites viewed this as laziness. Their racist views of African Americans permeated these codes, and in some cases, states just used the same wording they had used in the slave codes, this time using the word "Negro" instead of "slave."

Life in the South was very hard for the freed slaves. Besides the abuses they would receive because of their skin color, many could not find work. As a result, many of them became sharecroppers for white plantation owners. Sharecroppers were either black or poor white tenant farmers who rented their land from wealthy landowners. In essence, this is a form of slavery, and for many, their situation was not much better than it had been before the war. Other Black Codes made it criminal to be unemployed, in debt, vote, or have sex with a white woman. These codes legalized racism, giving birth to systemic racism in the United States, something which African Americans struggle with to this day. Using these codes as an excuse, the Ku Klux Klan terrorized blacks all across the South and Midwest. If a black person was arrested under these codes, they could be sentenced to forced labor, as it had been approved by the Thirteenth Amendment.

So regardless of the Thirteenth Amendment and the Civil Rights Act, blacks in the South essentially had no civil rights and lived in poverty. Some historians believe that many were worse off than when they were slaves.

The North was not blameless either. Some Northern politicians agreed with the reasoning behind the Black Codes, and some states even passed their own Black Codes. Indiana, Illinois, and Michigan all passed laws that banned the marriage of white and black people, something that all the Southern states had in place. Some Northern states had the same vagrancy laws as the South did, as well as laws that made black orphans available for whites to hire as a labor source. There was segregation, and for the most part, blacks were not able to vote.

In a large portion of the North and almost all of the South, the belief in white supremacy was embedded in the culture. In addition, many in the South took out their postwar anger on black people. The fact that blacks could be arrested for just being in a certain place (vagrancy) and forced into working for the whites led to a system of convict leasing. As this became more prominent, the South realized that it was more profitable to arrest black men and force them into labor. These men were essentially still slaves, just by a different name.

Chapter 7 – The Radical Reconstruction

The Reconstruction Act of 1867

In 1866, Northern voters reacted to the Presidential Reconstruction by voting in an overwhelmingly Radical Republican Congress. Given this increased power, Congress wrested the Reconstruction policies from the president.

Radical Reconstruction was also called Congressional Reconstruction, and it looked nothing like Johnson's Presidential Reconstruction. The Radical Republicans were determined to undo the lenient actions of President Johnson, and since they held enough control in both Houses of Congress to override any of Johnson's vetoes, they got to work. In March 1867, Congress passed the First Reconstruction Act of 1867.

In this act, the Confederate states were divided into military districts. It laid out how the Southern states would be governed, despite Johnson's earlier state conventions and reinstatements. Universal male suffrage was to be the law, and Confederate states would have to ratify the Fourteenth Amendment with all of its clauses intact, even though it infuriated the South. The Fourteenth Amendment was not a new bill; Congress had sent this amendment to the states for ratification in 1866 (it will be talked about in more detail in a separate chapter). Each state reentering the Union would also have state constitutions that mirrored the Thirteenth and Fourteenth Amendments. The Radical Republicans asserted the rights of black freedmen throughout the country, but especially in the South. In this environment, blacks would begin to participate in public life.

You can imagine the response of the ex-Confederates at this demand. After President Lincoln's and President Johnson's cooperative Reconstruction effort, this treatment must have come as a shock. It was demoralizing and depressing for white Southerners. And adding insult to injury, Congress demanded that each Confederate state ratify the Fourteenth Amendment, which clarified citizenship and the rights of citizens, and allow blacks to vote if they wanted to be part of the Union.

Many of these states had already agreed to Johnson's terms for reinstatement, and now they had to start all over again and rewrite their state constitution. This time around, they needed to incorporate the basic ideas of the Thirteenth and Fourteenth Amendments. The occupying Union troops were to oversee the voter registration of non-white men to ensure they had the right to vote.

When the Radical Republican Congress looked at the riots in New Orleans and Memphis, they determined that the Reconstruction was not harsh enough. Memphis saw its people turn against each other in May 1866. A large group of African Americans, mainly former veterans, gathered together and refused to disperse when asked by the police. Tensions escalated until two police officers had been shot. This incited a riot, with an angry mob of whites attacking blacks and burning down homes, schools, and churches. It is believed that forty-six African Americans and two European Americans died in the chaos. The New Orleans riots took place in late July of the same year. Black freedmen engaged in a peaceful demonstration, which was beset by white rioters. Between 30 and 50 blacks died, with around 150 wounded. It is believed that three whites also perished. Rather than see the riots as a message that Johnson's Reconstruction was too punitive, Congress pressed ahead, determined to enforce its will upon the South.

Although the white Southerners did not care for the Radical Reconstruction, the ex-slaves and the black community in general advanced somewhat. It was a much better situation than what Andrew Johnson's Presidential Reconstruction would have been. Still, it was not all positive. The white Southerners' strong and violent reactions greatly impacted the lives of black Southerners. For the most part, white Southerners ignored the laws that had been passed by Congress that granted rights to the ex-slaves. For African Americans, as well as the poor whites in the South, not much changed.

However, for a short time, the South experienced large scale interracial democracy. Black men could vote and run for office, winning seats in local and state governments and then winning seats on a federal level in Congress. This was due to the hidden agenda of the Republicans, which was to create a political stronghold in the South. By 1870, all the Confederate states had reunited with the Union, and the Republicans ran most of the state governments. Republican carpetbaggers, scalawags, and blacks made up the southern Republican Party, but by the end of the 1870s, the control was back in the hands of the Democrats. Jim Crow laws, poll taxes, the Ku Klux Klan, and many other factors would help to strip the blacks' rights away once again. However, in the beginning, there was a lot of advancement for blacks, especially in government.

It might be astonishing to some readers to hear how many blacks served in government during the Radical Reconstruction. More than 600 blacks served in state and local offices. The local offices they held were anything from the sheriff to the justice of the peace. And at least sixteen blacks served in the United States Congress. With blacks serving in local and state governments, public schools were established, laborers on plantations gained more bargaining power, and taxes were made more equitable. Racial discrimination in accommodations and public transportation was made illegal. The federal government supported the South with funding for railroads and new businesses. This was all good for the ex-slaves, but white Southerners felt more alienated and angrier with each passing day.

Chapter 8 – Carpetbaggers and Scallywags, 1867

After the Civil War came to a close, whites and, to an extent, blacks began to migrate south to promote the ideals the Radical Republicans were touting in Congress. In addition to them, there were also white Southerners who supported these efforts. These groups would come together to govern the South during the Radical Reconstruction. These governments were responsible for setting up charities, building schools, and improving infrastructure, namely shipping lanes and railroad transportation.

The people who came from the North were called carpetbaggers, regardless of race, while the white Southerners who supported the Radical Reconstruction were called scallywags. You might be wondering what is with the odd names. There was a lot of resentment among native white Southerners of every class toward the Northerners, who were essentially coming down to govern them. They were also angry at their own people for turning against them for an opportunity to advance further in government.

Following the Reconstruction Act of 1867, Southern governments were replaced by the Union military until new elections could be held. Freed slaves and freemen were able to vote and run in these elections. Those who held high positions in the Confederate government or military were stripped of their right to vote and hold office. These restrictions were later rescinded when all the Confederate states reentered the Union.

Due to these changes, blacks made up an overwhelming majority in the Republican Party of the South. Together with the Northern carpetbaggers and Southern scallywags, they were able to control most of the Southern legislatures and executive branches. Thus, whites and blacks governed together for the first time in the South.

Carpetbaggers

Who exactly were the carpetbaggers, and why did most Southerners resent or even hate their presence? The word "carpetbagger" gets its meaning from roaming individuals who arrive in a place they do not come from with only a carpetbag or satchel. Some opportunistic Northerners saw a chance after the war to move to the South and make their fortunes. White Southerners saw these people as outsiders and scoundrels, as they believed they were coming to exploit the people, whether it was in regards to money, land, or politics.

Carpetbaggers came to the South intending to buy land, partner with plantation owners who had no resources, or lease plantations. The carpetbaggers saw cotton as a way of making their fortune. After all, someone had to run the plantations and keep the economy going. However, to the established Southerner, the carpetbaggers were ruthless, opportunistic, lower-class whites who sought to make a fortune off their broken backs. There was tremendous resentment and scorn toward these Northerners as a result.

The truth was these Northerners were actually often middle class and well educated. They brought tremendous knowledge and resources to the South. They were businessmen, teachers, journalists, and merchants. Some were even with the Freedman's Bureau, and many had been soldiers in the Union Army. They considered themselves to be reformers who wanted to help build a new South in the model image of the North.

Scalawags

When the first Radical Reconstruction legislatures were set up in the South after the war, they were filled with white Southern Republicans. The Democrats referred to them as scalawags. It can also be spelled scallywag. The term is as old as the 1840s, and it refers to a farm animal that has no value but is taking up resources. Southerners used it to mean a worthless person, and this was exactly . how white Southerners saw their fellow Southerners who assisted or were loyal to the Union. In the white Southerners' eyes, a scalawag was much worse than a carpetbagger because they were from the South. Many considered them to be traitors.

Many scalawags were plantation owners or closeted abolitionists. They believed in black civil rights but also wanted to retain white control over the economy and political structures. Many of these Southern Republicans had been members of the Whig Party, which had fallen apart in 1854.

These Southerners believed they were better off joining the Republicans than being in opposition, as most of the South was. This group made up about 20 percent of the white voters in the South, and they came to hold a good deal of power in the local legislatures. Some had served in Congress or had been judges before the war.

The Radical Reconstruction

While Northerners were angry over Johnson's Presidential Reconstruction, many Southerners were mad at the Republicans for the Radical Reconstruction, as the Radical Reconstruction intended to undo what the Johnson Reconstruction had planned.

The Radical Reconstruction was based on the Republicans' view of freedom and equal rights, but Southerners hung on to their old worldview of slavery and free labor. As a result of their beliefs, the carpetbaggers and scallywags were easy scapegoats. They were labeled as scum and demeaned as being on the same level as the blacks. The Southern Democrats later used this rhetoric to rally the old South after the Republicans were defeated in 1877.

An editor of an Alabama paper defined the Reconstruction era scalawags, saying, "Our scalawag is the local leper of the community. Unlike the carpetbagger, he is native, which is so much worse. Once he was respected in his circle...and he could look his neighbor in the face. Now, possessed of the itch of office and the salt rheum of Radicalism, he is a mangy dog, slinking through the alleys, haunting the Governor's office, defiling with tobacco juice the steps of the Capitol, stretching his lazy carcass in the sun on the Square, or the benches of the Mayor's court." This viewpoint was quite prevalent, and it is easy to see how the scalawag came to be the hated symbol of the Radical Reconstruction.

Let's look beyond the stereotypes, though, and see what good these men created in the South. During the war, Union troops occupied the city of New Orleans. Once the war was over, there were still tens of thousands of Unionists in the city, including soldiers, planter lessees, and treasury agents. Many of these people stayed in New Orleans after the war, and they were seen as carpetbaggers by white Southerners. The first two governors after the Radical Reconstruction began were people that fell into this category. So were the three senators that Louisiana sent to Washington, DC, along with ten representatives. Oftentimes, the Speaker of the Louisiana House was a "carpetbagger."

These men had the knowledge and experience to run the newly configured state government. They ran the Post Office, the Internal Revenue Service, the Mint, the Customs House, the State Land Office, and the Fifth Circuit Federal Court. At the same time, Southern Democrats owned most of the land and ran most of the businesses, and the Ku Klux Klan targeted both scalawags and carpetbaggers.

Chapter 9 – The Fourteenth Amendment, 1868

Three years after the Thirteenth Amendment was ratified and two years after the Civil Rights Bill was passed, Congress was sitting on several pieces of legislation. One of them was an integral amendment of the US Constitution: the Fourteenth Amendment.

There are five sections to the Fourteenth Amendment. This amendment was often called the Reconstruction Amendment, and it gave us such familiar phrases as "due process" and "equal protection under the law."

It also cleared up the issue of representation to Congress. In the Constitution, slaves counted as three-fifths of a person. In the Thirteenth Amendment, ex-slaves became one person. Yet Congress still felt the need to add this clause to the Fourteenth Amendment: "Representation shall be apportioned among the several states according to the respective numbers, counting the whole number of persons in each state, excluding Indians not taxed." Representation to Congress continues to be apportioned in this manner today.

Let's take a look at the clauses of the Fourteenth Amendment in closer detail. It certainly starts off with a bang. "All persons born or naturalized in the United States...are citizens of the United States and of the State wherein they reside." With these words, Congress made it clear that ex-slaves and their children were automatically citizens of the United States. If they had been born in Africa, there was a process for becoming a naturalized citizen.

This section goes on to say, "No State shall make or enforce any law which shall abridge the privileges and immunities of citizens." But what exactly were those privileges? It hearkens back to a phrase most Americans are familiar with today—life, liberty, and property. Sounds pretty familiar to the words set down by the Founding Fathers almost 100 years before. The Fourteenth Amendment also stated that citizens should not be deprived of the "due process of law; nor deny to any person within its jurisdiction the equal protection of the laws."

The keywords here are "due process of law" and "equal protection of the laws." In fact, they might be the most important phrases in the amendment. In all the years since the Civil War, Americans have hung their liberty on the Due Process Clause and the Equal Protection Clause. Many Americans take these rights for granted today, but they were bombshells to the American people back in the late 1800s.

The next section of the Fourteenth Amendment covers the allocation of representatives; as mentioned above, the Three-Fifths Compromise was no longer in effect, and everyone counted as one person (excluding Native Americans). But more importantly, this section gave all black men the right to vote in the country.

> But when the right to vote at any election...is denied to any of the male inhabitants of such State, being twenty-one years of age, and citizens of the United States, or in any way abridged, except for participation in rebellion, or other crime, the basis of representation [in regards to the number of state representatives to Congress] therein shall be reduced in the

proportion which the number of such male citizens shall bear to the whole number of male citizens twenty-one years of age in such State.

The next section addressed the issue of Confederate generals and politicians who sought a government position in the United States government. The clause doesn't refer to the Confederate states in particular; rather, it states that no one who had "previously taken an oath" (as in a loyalty oath to serve the country) and then "engaged in insurrection or rebellion...or given aid or comfort to the enemies thereof" could hold office. This was a very punitive clause as far as the South was concerned. However, the amendment made a concession, saying that if two-thirds of Congress approved of someone, they would be allowed to take office.

In the fourth section, the public debt acquired throughout the war was validated. However, the United States did not hold itself responsible for the debt. "Neither the United States nor any State shall assume or pay any debt or obligation incurred in aid of insurrection or rebellion...or any claim for the loss or emancipation of any slave." The important phrase in this section is "or any claim for the loss or emancipation of any slave." In other words, no slave owner in the South would be compensated in any way for income or personal loss due to the freeing of the slaves. Remember, Lincoln and Johnson most likely would have approached this differently. Radical Republicans wanted nothing to do with compensating slave owners for what they considered to be an immoral act. In addition, the Fourteenth Amendment stated that the war debt was void. No state governments or even the federal government would reimburse the Confederate states for any war losses.

Finally, the amendment ends with "The Congress shall have the power to enforce, by appropriate legislation, the provisions of this article." Maybe you want to read that again. The Fourteenth Amendment, which was designed to complete the Radical

Reconstruction, had a way to reach through the centuries of American law and jurisprudence.

On June 16th, 1866, the Fourteenth Amendment was sent to the states for ratification. It took over two years for enough states to ratify it, and it was finally adopted on July 9th, 1868. Its purpose was to ensure equal civil rights for the emancipated slaves when it was adopted. Unfortunately, the South found ways around this for decades by using the notorious Black Codes, Jim Crow laws, and the future Supreme Court ruling of *Plessy v. Ferguson.*

The Fourteenth Amendment was the second of the three amendments that helped to abolish slavery and/or grant basic civil rights to the freed slaves and all blacks throughout the Union. The Fourteenth Amendment rejected the 1857 Dred Scott decision of the United States Supreme Court. That decision said that black men, born free or otherwise emancipated, did not share the same rights as whites according to the US Constitution. What this decision had denied to blacks, the Fourteenth Amendment granted to them.

After more than a century of the balance of power favoring the states, this amendment shifted that balance toward the federal government. This amendment is also the foundation of the Civil Rights Act of 1964 and the Voting Rights Act of 1965. Yet, if this amendment had been implemented to its fullest to begin with, those laws might never have been needed.

Before this amendment, the Supreme Court tended to rule in favor of the states on the questions of civil rights. After this amendment, the Supreme Court tended to rule in favor of maintaining the individual's civil rights. But this did not happen overnight. For instance, the *Plessy v. Ferguson* decision in 1896 was used for decades to validate the Jim Crow laws in the South.

Court Decisions Influenced by the Fourteenth Amendment

The Due Process Clause stated that not only did the federal government owe a citizen the due process of the law but so did the states. This Due Process Clause has been ruled on many times by the Supreme Court, expanding US citizens' rights almost every time. The Supreme Court has used this clause to protect individuals from infringement by states or the federal government.

The Equal Protection Clause and the Due Process Clause have been cited by the Supreme Court to expand protections for everything from the Bill of Rights to the right to privacy to the right to marry. The Equal Protection Clause was intended to keep the states from either legislating or approving of discrimination against blacks, and both of these clauses became the bulwarks for many landmark decisions.

Let's take a quick look at some of the Supreme Court's most important decisions that were influenced by these two clauses of the Fourteenth Amendment.

1925 – In *Gitlow v. New York*, the Supreme Court ruled that the Fourteenth Amendment extended the rights of the First Amendment, such as freedom of speech and freedom of the press, to state governments.

1954 – *Brown v. Board of Education* was a landmark case regarding civil rights. This case overturned the ruling of *Plessy v. Ferguson*, which stated "separate but equal." By using the Fourteenth Amendment, the Supreme Court declared that segregation in public schools did not meet the Equal Protection Clause's standards.

1965 – *Griswold v. Connecticut* paved the way for women to use contraception legally. This might seem like an odd case in regards to the Fourteenth Amendment, but a Supreme Court justice argued for the ruling by referring to the Due Process Clause, which protects the right to privacy.

1967 – *Loving v. Virginia* was another landmark case. The Supreme Court ruled that laws banning interracial marriage violated the Fourteenth Amendment and was unconstitutional.

1973 – This was the year the Supreme Court ruled on one of the most controversial cases it ever faced. The case was *Roe v. Wade*, and by using the Due Process Clause in the Fourteenth Amendment, the court found that laws against abortion violated a women's right to privacy. However, it left the book open on this by saying this right is not absolute and that it has to be balanced with the government's interests in protecting women's health and prenatal life.

2015 –*Obergefell v. Hodges* was another landmark decision. The Supreme Court ruled that the clauses in the Fourteenth Amendment upheld the right for same-sex couples to marry on the same terms as opposite-sex couples.

The Supreme Court has ruled that there are three protections provided by the Due Process Clause. They are:

1. Substantive Due Process – This allows courts to protect certain fundamental rights, even if they are not mentioned in the US Constitution.

2. Procedural Due Process – At its most basic definition, procedural due process means providing the person with notice, an opportunity to be heard, and a neutral person's decision. Many in the US are familiar with the Miranda warning; this is used to ensure procedural due process is being followed accordingly.

3. Vehicle for incorporating the Bill of Rights – Initially, the Supreme Court said that the Bill of Rights only applied to the federal government. However, they later ruled that the provisions in the Bill of Rights did apply to the states through the doctrine of incorporation in the Due Process Clause of the Fourteenth Amendment.

There has also been much debate regarding the citizenship clause over the years. Were children of immigrants automatically citizens? Was anyone born in the United States with parents that held citizenship elsewhere automatically a citizen? What about children born in the United States to diplomats from other countries? In the first two instances, the Supreme Court ruled that these children were citizens. However, a child born to foreign diplomats is not an automatic citizen. The Foreign Affairs Manual from the State Department makes it clear that "U.S. military installations abroad and U.S. diplomatic or consular facilities abroad are not part of the United States within the meaning of the Fourteenth Amendment."

By passing and ratifying the Fourteenth Amendment in 1868, the Radical Republican Congress believed they were addressing the Reconstruction's current needs. They had no idea of the amendment's importance when it came to shaping the future of the country and the validity of civil rights. Without this amendment, there may not have been a Civil Rights Act and a Voting Rights Act in the 1960s. Without this amendment, there would not have been the reading of the Miranda rights. Without this amendment, there might have been no right to privacy and no right to marry whoever you choose. It is unlikely the Radical Republicans had any inkling about the road they were setting the country on; however, due to the precedent they set, civil rights continued to move forward. Sadly, during their own time, civil rights stagnated, and although important bills were passed, they were never utilized to their fullest limits.

Chapter 10 – The Impeachment of Andrew Johnson, 1868

Many people are aware that Andrew Johnson was impeached by the House of Representatives and acquitted by the Senate. However, most of us do not understand why or what happened to instigate this action.

After Johnson declared Reconstruction to be over, Congress, which was run by the Radical Republicans, challenged him at every step. First, they created the Joint Committee on Reconstruction. Then they passed the Civil Rights Act of 1866 and the second Freedmen's Bureau bill, both of which the president vetoed. He also vetoed numerous Reconstruction Acts. However, Congress overruled him at almost every turn. As you can tell, there was much antagonism between the president and the sitting congressmen.

The passages of these bills and amendments angered white Southerners, which led to riots throughout the South. Many innocent former slaves were killed. Angry Northerners blamed President Johnson for this, believing he was too soft on the South.

Johnson proceeded to travel throughout the country, blaming the Radical Republicans, the blacks, and the pro-war Democrats for the ills of the reunited Union. This press tour is often referred to as Johnson's "Swing Around the Circle." This effort failed, however, as it turned more Northerners to the Republicans in the 1866 elections. The Northerners were angry with Johnson for his pardons to Southern leaders and the fact that it seemed like blacks in the South were still "slaves," as the freed slaves were often working on the same plantations where they had once labored in the fields without any pay.

But what does all this have to do with the impeachment of Johnson? The actions of the House of Representatives were firmly rooted in the intense animosity between President Johnson and the Republican Congress. Congress continued to pass laws giving rights to freed slaves and restricting the activity of the South, while Johnson continued to veto them. Though the Republicans often had the votes to override Johnson's vetoes, they grew more irritated with his presidency every day. They looked for ways to fight back and eventually passed the Tenure of Office Act in 1867, which limited some presidential powers.

The Tenure of Office Act was actually passed in regards to Edward Stanton, the Secretary of War, who was a Radical Republican. Stanton had been Lincoln's choice for the position of secretary of war, so Johnson inherited him. Johnson inherited many Republicans, but none stood in his way as much as Stanton did. Congress was worried Stanton would be replaced, so they passed this act in 1867 to ensure he wouldn't be dismissed without reason. This act called for the president to seek the Senate's consent before dismissing any members of his Cabinet.

Johnson tried to force Stanton's resignation but failed to do so. In the summer of 1867, while Congress was in recess, President Johnson suspended Stanton, and Ulysses S. Grant was chosen to take his place. This move was allowed under the Tenure of Office Act, but it was something that Congress was not expecting. When the Senate met back up later that year, they said they did not concur with the decision. Grant said he would resign, as he feared a legal battle would ensue, but Johnson convinced him to stay. When the Senate voted to reinstate Stanton in January of the next year, Grant immediately stepped to the side, leading to a breakdown between him and Johnson. However, it was due to these actions that Grant became the frontrunner for the 1868 presidential election, which he would go on to win.

Johnson searched for someone else to fill the spot, but instead of compromising, he simply chose someone who he knew would be loyal to him. The interim secretary of war, Lorenzo Thomas, hand-delivered Stanton's dismissal letter to him, but Stanton refused to leave his post, citing the Tenure of Office Act.

The Senate was outraged. The president had challenged a congressional order, and the House of Representatives quickly wrote up articles of impeachment, charging Johnson with "high crimes and misdemeanors."

The House voted to impeach 126 to 47, but the majority of the Senate voted for acquittal. Johnson survived by one single vote. At that time, Johnson did not have a vice president. If he had been removed from office, the Senate's pro tempore would have been next in line for the presidency, unlike today when the Speaker of the House would ascend to the presidency.

Andrew Johnson was the first of only three US presidents to be impeached (so far, no US president has been convicted on these terms). The political implications of this action shifted the balance of power again between the executive and legislative branches. Congress could not impeach a president just because they didn't like his policies. But, at the same time, the impeachment diminished the president's power.

There were other fallouts from the impeachment trial. No Republican senator who voted to acquit ever served in public office again, and Johnson's presidency was essentially over. The Tenure of Office Act was repealed in 1887, and the Supreme Court deemed the act to be unconstitutional in 1926 during the case of *Myers v. United States.*

Chapter 11 – The Fifteenth Amendment, 1870

Ulysses S. Grant was elected president in 1868, although he wouldn't take office until the following March. There was a lot of concern in the Republican Party regarding their possible success in future elections. Most Republicans believed that the Democrats would see a resurgence, and they knew they needed the black vote to stay in power.

So, on February 26th, 1869, Congress passed a compromised version of the Fifteenth Amendment. The final version banned any restrictions on voting based on race, color, or previous servitude.

However, the amendment was a far cry from the original wording. Representative John Bingham, who helped draft the Fourteenth Amendment, pushed for an amendment that included bans on the basis of "race, color, nativity, property, education, or religious beliefs." There was also a clause to ban literacy tests. Prejudice was strong everywhere, not just in the South. The North had an influx of foreign-born citizens, and some House representatives (both in the North and in the West) did not want them to be able to easily vote. In addition, both Southern and Northern Republicans wanted those Southerners who had supported the Confederacy to still be banned from voting;

they believed this amendment would make it easier for them to gain their right to vote.

Because of all the infighting, the House and the Senate passed different versions of the amendment, which meant that a House and Senate conference committee had to meet to hammer out the differences and produce the amendment's final wording. In the interest of getting the amendment ratified by the necessary number of states, the more controversial language, such as guaranteeing blacks could hold office or banning poll taxes, were not included.

The House approved of the new wording on February 25th, 1869, with the Senate approving the measure the next day. The House saw 35 representatives abstain from voting, while 144 members voted for it. Forty-four members voted against it. The vote in the Senate was 39 to 13, with 14 senators abstaining. Thirteen Radical Republican senators refused to vote because the amendment was not what they had envisioned, and they wanted something that would benefit blacks more. Despite this, the amendment passed.

The wording of the amendment is short and simple, but its impact has been felt down through the years. Much blood, tears, and heartbreak has been shed and felt because of it. The amendment simply states:

> Section 1. The right of citizens of the United States to vote shall not be denied or abridged by the United States or by any State on account of race, color, or previous condition of servitude.

> Section 2. The Congress shall have power to enforce this article by appropriate legislation.

Opposition to this amendment also came from the women's suffrage movement. Before and during the Civil War, the women's suffrage movement had been aligned with the abolitionist movement. The Fourteenth Amendment left women feeling that their rights were not important, as only male rights were protected. Some women wanted to continue their work and make sure African Americans got the equality they deserved, while other prominent women, such as Susan B. Anthony and Elizabeth Cady Stanton, wanted rights extended to women at the same time.

Things got worse with the proposal of the Fifteenth Amendment because it barred race discrimination but not sex discrimination. This caused a rift in the movement, as the women now knew they had to choose which issue to prioritize first. This split the American Equal Rights Association in two. The new organizations became rivals, with the National Woman Suffrage Association, led by Susan B. Anthony and Elizabeth Cady Stanton, rejecting the Fifteenth Amendment. The American Woman Suffrage Association, led by Lucy Stone and an African American woman named Frances Ellen Watkins Harper, supported the amendment.

But the amendment wouldn't be a reality until enough states ratified it. On March 1ˢᵗ, 1869, Nevada became the first state to ratify the Fifteenth Amendment. Within a few months, most of the Midwestern and New England states had ratified it as well. Some of the Southern states in which the Radical Republicans still had control also ratified it quickly.

To get the last few needed states, Congress passed several Reconstruction acts that made it mandatory for the states of Virginia, Mississippi, Texas, and Georgia to ratify the amendment before sending representatives to Congress again. By February 1870, all four states had ratified the amendment. On February 3ʳᵈ, 1870, twenty-eight states had ratified the amendment, and it became a part of the Constitution. Iowa was the last of the twenty-eight states to do so, following the example of Georgia, which had passed it just the day before.

Abolitionist organizations and black communities celebrated, as many considered this event to be the end of Reconstruction and a moment where black rights were secured for future generations. The Republicans were so confident that they even proclaimed black men no longer needed the federal government's protection. Many abolitionist organizations disbanded, and James A. Garfield, who would later become the president, said the amendment's passage "confers upon the African race the care of its destiny. It places their fortunes in their own hands." Unfortunately, they were wrong. It was certainly a major accomplishment for black civil rights, but it was not the end of their story, nor was it the end of Reconstruction.

It was still a great moment in history when, on March 31ˢᵗ, 1870, Thomas Mundy Peterson cast his vote in New Jersey, becoming the first black man to vote due to the provisions of the Fifteenth Amendment. This was followed by the election of many blacks to public office, as black men took advantage of their newly protected rights. Around 2,000 black men held local, state, and federal offices throughout the country, with sixteen serving in Congress.

While the Fifteenth Amendment granted black men the right to vote, states, particularly in the South, made it difficult for them to cast their ballot. This can be seen in the following court cases, which required the US Supreme Court to weigh in.

Judicial Reviews

1876 - *United States v. Reese* was probably the most important case in regards to the limitations that would be placed on blacks in the years to come. In 1873, two election inspectors refused to allow an African American man to vote in an election in Kentucky. They stated that the man had refused to pay the poll tax, even though the man had tried to pay it but was refused. They also refused his affidavit, which would have excused the non-paid poll tax under the Enforcement Act of 1870 (this act prohibited officials from discriminating against those trying to vote based on race or color). The two election inspectors were charged with violating the Enforcement Act, but instead of reinforcing that act, the Supreme Court decided the wording in the Enforcement Act was too broad and didn't fit in the context of the Fifteenth Amendment. The justices interpreted the amendment much more narrowly. They ruled that the Fifteenth Amendment didn't actually "grant the right of suffrage"; rather, it prohibited the states "from giving preference...to one citizen of the United States over another on account of race, color, or previous condition of servitude...If citizens of one race having certain qualifications are permitted by law to vote, those of another having the same qualifications must be."

This ruling led to states, particularly in the South, to pass laws that excluded blacks, as well as poor white men, from voting. Literacy tests and poll taxes became commonplace over time. Grandfather clauses were also in place in some states, which exempted voters from these voting requirements if their grandfathers had been able to vote. These measures were not limited to the South. This Supreme Court ruling also led the Ku Klux Klan and other white supremacists to use violence and intimidation to keep blacks from voting, which will be covered in more depth in the next chapter.

As the Supreme Court continued to interpret the Fifteenth Amendment more narrowly, Southern states adopted new constitutions and new laws to set conditions for voting registration. It was not until the early 1900s that the Supreme Court began to give a broader interpretation to the Fifteenth Amendment.

1915 - In *Guinn v. the United States*, the Supreme Court struck down the grandfather clause that had allowed whites, especially those who were poorer and illiterate, to bypass poll taxes and literacy tests.

1927 - The Supreme Court struck down a Texas law that forbade blacks from voting in the Texas Democratic primary in *Nixon v. Herndon*. Dr. Lawrence Nixon, who was African American, would later bring another case to the Supreme Court in 1932, which again challenged the idea of an all-white Democratic primary in Texas. It was only in 1944, in *Smith v. Allwright*, that white primaries in Texas were deemed unconstitutional, which, in turn, affected other states.

1960 - *Gomillion v. Lightfoot* ruled that a gerrymandered district, which aimed to exclude black voters, violated the Fifteenth Amendment. Gerrymandering is not a thing of the past, as it still happens today, but redrawing lines to disenfranchise racial and ethnic minorities is not allowed. While Gerrymandering based on party lines is allowed, many argue that this is a fine line, as they can still affect racial and ethnic minorities.

This amendment continued to play a major role in validating the civil rights acts in the 1960s. For instance, in 1965, Congress passed the Voting Rights Act. This act addressed many of the ways that Southern states had disenfranchised black voters, despite the rights laid out in previous amendments. The Voting Rights Act outlawed literacy tests and established the federal government's oversight of voter registration in the areas where the majority of black residents were not registered. It also allowed the US attorney general to investigate other disenfranchisement tools, such as the poll tax.

Chapter 12 – The Ku Klux Klan Act, 1871

Most people have seen the pictures and heard the stories. Out of the darkness of the night would come hooded horseman or people on foot, who would then burn crosses in front of houses, beat up unsuspecting blacks, and terrorize the black community by hanging black men from trees. These masked men were known as the Ku Klux Klan or, more simply as, the KKK.

In late December 1865, former Confederate officers of the Civil War founded a secret social fraternity named the Ku Klux Klan. The Klan did not stay a social fraternity for long, as it soon warped into a violent terror group with a paramilitary attitude. The Klan's goal was to reverse everything the federal government had achieved during Reconstruction. Their main focus was to repress the rights of former slaves and all black people.

But why the name Ku Klux Klan? It is thought they used the Greek word *kyklos*, meaning circle, in combination with the word "clan." For a short time, the Klan was known as the Kuklux Clan. The first grand wizard of the KKK was a former confederate general named Nathan Bedford Forrest. Forrest eventually tired of the Klan's violence and tried to disband it, although he was unsuccessful. Late in life, he claimed he had never even been a part of the organization, although this claim is false.

Black Americans were not the only ones targeted by the Klan. Anyone who assisted them or stood up for them was also vulnerable. This was particularly true of white Republicans living in the South. The Klan destroyed property and assaulted and murdered their victims to intimidate blacks from voting in elections.

When the Union soldiers were still in the South, they could break up the Klan activities. In 1870, Congress passed the First Ku Klux Act (also known as the Enforcement Act). This act prohibited discrimination in regards to voting. This act even gave the president the right to deploy the military if rebellions broke out due to this act. The Second Enforcement Act was passed in 1871, and it continued to help protect the voting rights of African Americans.

The last Enforcement Act (known as the Third Enforcement Act, the Third Ku Klux Klan Act, or simply the Ku Klux Klan Act) was also passed in 1871. This piece of legislation gave the president the authority to suspend the writ of *habeas corpus* (under which people could report unlawful imprisonment to a court) in order to fight the Klan and other white supremacist groups. It was brought to the House by Republican Representative Samuel Shellabarger from Ohio, and it passed the House on April 6th. It was amended and then sent to the Senate, where it passed, becoming law on April 20th, 1871.

Opponents of the bill considered it unconstitutional, as they believed it violated the rights of state governments to control their elections. Others expressed the opposite sentiments, as the violence of the Klan and other white supremacist groups were incredibly harmful to the American public, particularly the black populace. Six months after signing the bill into law, Grant used its provisions in South Carolina. Martial law was declared in nine South Carolina counties, and the military arrested hundreds of alleged Klansmen. Due to this move, the Klan disappeared in South Carolina and elsewhere in the South.

If you try to find this act in its entirety today, you won't find it. The act has undergone many revisions, with portions of the act expiring after the Reconstruction. The Supreme Court's narrow interpretation also impacted the effects of the law, as most of their rulings stated that the law only applied to the states. In 1883, the Supreme Court found some of this legislation to be unconstitutional.

By that time, though, the Klan had faded into the background, although it would come back years later in 1915, this time with a focus on persecuting not just blacks but also Catholics, Jews, and immigrants. This revival would slowly fade away in the 1940s before rising yet again in full force in the 1950s and 1960s to fight the civil rights movement. Some chapters of the Ku Klux Klan have survived to this day, and there is a movement to label the group as a terrorist organization.

Chapter 13 – The Civil Rights Act of 1875

Three years after the passage of the Ku Klux Klan Act, Congress felt the need for another act to help protect African American civil rights and passed the Civil Rights Act of 1875. Once again, Congress was attempting to enforce the rights of all citizens, particularly those that were outlined in the Thirteenth, Fourteenth, and Fifteenth Amendments.

This act was drafted by Radical Republican Senator Charles Sumner and John Mercer Langston, an African American who would become the first president of Virginia State University and the first dean at Howard University. The last name of Langston might sound familiar to some; his brother was the grandfather of the well-known poet Langston Hughes. Although the bill was drafted in 1870, it did not get passed until 1875. By this time, Sumner had died, and many saw the act as a way to memorialize his work. Although Grant signed the law, he didn't agree with it. He and Sumner had never seen eye to eye, and Grant did nothing to ensure the law was enforced effectively. The federal government did not send copies to United States attorneys around the country, and federal courts ruled that it was unconstitutional long before the US Supreme Court issued their ruling. Public opinion on the bill was split right down the color line, with whites opposing it and blacks supporting it. It was overwhelmingly opposed in newspaper editorials around the country.

The law was intended to provide equal treatment to all citizens in regards to public transportation and to stop blacks from being excluded from jury service. It also included a clause that stated any lawsuits coming from civil rights violations must be heard in federal courts, not state or local courts. However, Grant had wanted a law that would help suppress the violence related to black voting rights in the South. The Reconstruction was on its last legs by this point, and it would end about two years later. The Civil Rights Act of 1875 would be the last major piece of legislation related to Reconstruction.

The law read, in part, "all persons within the jurisdiction of the United States shall be entitled to the full and equal enjoyment of the accommodations, advantages, facilities, and privileges of inns, public conveyances on land or water, theaters, and other places of public amusement; subject only to the conditions and limitations established by law, and applicable alike to citizens of every race and color."

As you can see, the public accommodation clause was at the heart of the act. Unfortunately, the Supreme Court ruled this section of the act unconstitutional in 1883 in the *Civil Rights Cases*, which was a group of five cases related to civil rights. The Supreme Court said the Equal Protection Clause of the Fourteenth Amendment, which this bill enforced, did not prohibit discrimination by individuals or organizations. It only prohibits local or state governments from discriminating. They also ruled that the Thirteenth Amendment was meant to ensure blacks were no longer seen as slaves; according to the majority of the justices, it did not have anything to do with discrimination in public accommodations. Thus, segregation would remain in place until the 1960s. In 1964 and 1968, two new acts were passed, and parts of the Civil Rights Act of 1875 were incorporated into them.

Long-Term Impact

As noted above, this was the last major piece of civil rights legislation during the Reconstruction era. In fact, it would be the last federal civil rights act until 1957.

It appears that the public in the North and the South had grown tired of the Reconstruction. They wanted it over with, even if that meant embracing segregation. However, blacks saw this act as an important piece of legislation. In 1874, while the bill was being debated in the House of Representatives, African American Representative James Rapier from Alabama stood up and said, "I have no compromise to offer on this subject...After all, this question resolves itself into this: either I am a man or I am not a man."

Even though this act had little impact when it was enacted, it would find new life almost ninety years later in the 1960s with the passage of some of the most influential civil rights acts.

Chapter 14 – The Compromise of 1877

The politics of 1877 were drastically different from when the Radical Republicans took over Congress and impeached Andrew Johnson back in the late 1860s. This was perfectly exemplified by the elections of 1877. By this year, people in both the North and the South were tired and wanted the Reconstruction to be over, and there was little support for any more legislation for advantageous racially inspired policies.

Southern whites were more than fed up with the Reconstruction and still used violence and intimidation to prevent blacks from voting, serving on juries, or using public accommodations. Northerners had other things on their plates that they thought needed to be prioritized. The Gilded Age was beginning to bloom, and with that came new business ventures and labor strikes; issues of the economy were coming to the forefront, while civil rights were getting pushed back. Many white Northerners thought they had done enough to secure liberties for blacks. They thought the issue now lay with Southern governments. Others thought it could not be achieved, as their efforts often led to violence and the dissolution of their policies. The Supreme Court struck down many provisions of the Thirteenth and

Fourteenth Amendments and narrowly interpreted other acts; it seemed this would be a never-ending battle. There were also many accusations of corruption within the Grant administration, which made an already weary public turn against the Republican Party, which had been in power since Lincoln was inaugurated in 1861.

Of course, the problem with leaving the cause of civil rights in the hands of the South was that many white Southerners did not care about the advancement of African Americans, which was reflected in government politics. Regardless, by 1877, there was just no appetite left in the North for fighting these inequities.

Before the Compromise of 1877

Throughout the 19th century, America was a country of compromises in an attempt to blend the very different worlds of slavery and non-slavery and of the agricultural South and the industrial North. Parts of the country threatened to secede numerous times during the century, and every time except for one, the government was able to make compromises that prevented the nation from splitting apart.

The compromises can be seen in the US government's earliest history. Right from the start—within the Constitution itself—these compromises were front and center. This compromise was reached in 1787 during the Constitutional Convention. The convention's delegates had argued bitterly over the issue of slavery and the question of congressional representation. The North did not want the South to be able to count their slaves toward the population, which would be used to determine congressional representation. Of course, the South demanded to count all persons, including the slaves. The North believed that this would give the South an unfair allocation due to the many enslaved people in the South.

This was a major roadblock to passing the Constitution, and a compromise had to be reached. Eventually, the delegates came up with the Three-Fifths Compromise, in which the slaves in the South were to be counted as three-fifths of a person for the purposes of congressional representation. Another way of looking at it was to count three out of every five slaves. And yet another way of looking at it is that the American public, for the most part, actually saw slaves as three-fifths of a person. This completely dehumanized the slave population, and it took over one hundred years for America to realize what had been "best" for the American public in 1787 was no longer the case. Of course, it was not best for the slaves or the black population in general, and sadly, this mentality was passed down through the generations.

Another significant compromise regarding slavery was the Missouri Compromise of 1820. The Missouri Compromise was another attempt to keep the Union together. As Missouri moved to become a state, many involved simply assumed it would be a pro-slavery state. However, many abolitionists and Republicans vigorously fought against another slave state from entering the Union. After much wrangling, Congress passed the Missouri Compromise. The compromise allowed Missouri to enter the Union as a slave state but banned all slavery north of the 36° 30' parallel. This compromise was enacted after President James Monroe signed it in 1820.

The next major compromise was the Compromise of 1850. The Compromise of 1850 actually refers to five different bills. These dealt with the land the United States had acquired with its victory in the Mexican-American War. This territory included the modern-day states of New Mexico, Arizona, Utah, Nevada, California, and a part of Colorado. Once again, the question of slavery found its way to the top of this discussion. California would be admitted as a free state, while the other territories would have to figure out their stance on slavery. The Compromise of 1850 also reinforced the Fugitive Slave Act of 1793. Law enforcement was supposed to arrest anyone suspected of being a fugitive slave. Anyone who did not arrest an alleged fugitive slave would be subjected to a fine, as would those aiding runaway slaves.

The final compromise before the Civil War broke out was the Nebraska-Kansas Act. In 1854, the Nebraska-Kansas Act was passed to open up these lands for the transcontinental railroad. However, it is most remembered for repealing the Missouri Compromise of 1820.

Since it no longer mattered if a state was above or below the 36° 30' parallel, both anti-slavery and pro-slavery advocates moved to Kansas in an effort to be the deciding populace regarding slavery in the new state. These battles between pro-slavery and anti-slavery groups grew more violent, eventually resulting in Bleeding Kansas. Kansas would be admitted as a free state in 1861, but many in the nation knew that the issue of slavery would lead to war, just as it had in Kansas.

The Compromise of 1877

The Compromise of 1877 was different than the others that came before it in two ways.

> 1. It was put in place after the Civil War. All the other compromises had been reached before the war in an attempt to prevent the Southern states from seceding. It is interesting to note that this compromise had the same goal as the first three—to hold the Union together.

> 2. The Compromise of 1877 was not worked out in the halls of Congress with vigorous debates and passionate speeches. No, this compromise was worked on behind closed doors. It was the result of a disputed and chaotic presidential election, during which both the North and the South accused each other of fraud. Old issues had reared their ugly heads to taint the election's results.

The presidential election of 1876 was filled with much tension. Many thought Grant would run for a third time, and when he decided not to do so, there was a mad dash to find a strong candidate. That candidate was Rutherford B. Hayes, and he went up against Democratic candidate Samuel Tilden. The number of electoral votes needed at that time was 185. Tilden ended up with 184 electoral votes, while Hayes had 165. The problem was that the remaining four states who had to report their counts were struck by voter fraud. For instance, in South Carolina, 101 percent of voters cast a vote. Tilden had a huge lead in the popular vote, but the Republicans refused to concede. They claimed fraud had occurred in the South, as both African Americans and Republicans were intimidated into not voting. The voting in South Carolina was marred with violence on both sides. Clashes between whites and blacks resulted in the deaths of five people. In a town near Charleston, violence took the lives of six white men when black men opened fire inside a political meeting.

While three of the contested states were in the South, the other one was in the West. Oregon's electoral vote seemed to be in Hayes's favor, but the governor claimed that one of the electors was ineligible, replacing the former Republican elector with a Democratic one. All of this threw the election into chaos. As a result, Rutherford B. Hayes became the first and so far the only president ever to be decided by an Electoral Commission.

Before getting into the specifics of the Compromise of 1877, it is interesting to look at who scholars think won the election. It is certainly hard to know for certain, as the election was not conducted fairly in the South, but more than likely, Hayes would have won Oregon, South Carolina, and Louisiana, while Tilden would have won Florida. If this had been the case, scholars think Hayes would have won not only the electoral vote but also the popular vote.

Here is what happened when the Democrats and Republicans met in private at the Wormley Hotel in Washington, DC. In order to give the election to Hayes, it is believed the Democrats demanded:

> • The removal of all federal troops from Louisiana, South Carolina, and Florida. This move would effectively end the Reconstruction, as all Southern states would then be under home rule.

- The appointment of a Southern Democrat to the Cabinet. Hayes appointed an ex-Confederate as the postmaster general. This move was not popular in the North or with the Northern Republicans, who still controlled the Senate.

- The provision of federal funds and assistance to industrialize the South in an attempt to boost the Southern economy. Southern ports were still devastated, and even Mississippi River shipping was down to nothing.

- The federal government would provide funding for a transcontinental railway across the South.

- The federal government would not interfere with racial issues in the South. This might have been the point that had the most ramifications over the decades.

It is not known for certain what deals were made at the Wormley Hotel, but scholars are fairly certain these were the key points. Regardless, the inauguration of Rutherford Hayes, which took place peacefully on March 5th, 1877, effectively ended the Reconstruction.

Although Hayes said he was committed to a Southern route for the railroad, he did not keep this promise. However, Southern Democrats did not live up to their commitment to "recognize the civil and political equality of blacks." The Democrats in the South proceeded to pass various taxes and laws that greatly affected African Americans. Blacks felt that the Republican Party had betrayed them, as the South fell under Democratic rule until the 1960s.

Was the Compromise of 1877 worth the price each side paid? Was the presidency worth giving up the fight for equal rights? Most Republicans thought so. It seems their thinking was short-sighted. A president typically served eight years (two terms) back then, but safeguarding civil rights, especially according to our modern viewpoint, would have been the heroic and right thing to do. After this election, the Democrats would own the "Solid South" until the 1980s, which was when the Republicans again took over. It should be noted that over time, the two parties also slowly switched values. Most scholars believe this started to happen in 1936 when Franklin Delano Roosevelt, a Democrat, was re-elected for the second time. The Democratic Party, which used to advocate for a strong state government, began advocating for a strong central government, in addition to increased civil rights.

However, the compromise of 1877 did keep the Union in one piece, but nothing would be the same. Democrats learned quickly that the old South before the war was not coming back, and it also did not bring the South onto equal terms with the North regarding the economy, social order, and political standing. However, it did dictate that white rule and influence would prevail in the South for generations to come. This rule was held together by the oppression, intimidation, and segregation of the millions of African Americans who lived in those states.

In 1877, the military forces of the North left the South, which resulted in widespread disenfranchisement of blacks and the new Jim Crow laws. Segregation ruled in the South until Lyndon Baines Johnson's administration took over following President John F. Kennedy's assassination.

Chapter 15 – The Official End of the Reconstruction

The end of Reconstruction wasn't pretty. It wasn't well organized. And it wasn't planned. You could say the country had simply grown weary of the Reconstruction efforts and wanted it to be over. The anger and bitterness caused by the Civil War had essentially subsided, and Republicans began to back away from their commitments to racial equality in the South and the broad powers of the federal government that was needed to accomplish it.

Over time, the Republicans had become less "radical" and more conservative. For many Republicans, the Radical Reconstruction looked like a misguided adventure. To them, it seemed like a time filled with failed attempts to raise the standard of living for blacks and the poor in the South. Thus, the Republicans in 1876 and 1877 began to see the Reconstruction as a fading era and chose to abandon it.

As the Republicans backed away, white Democratic local and state governments began to take over. Many complained that the Reconstruction had banned the leaders of the Confederacy—both civilian and military—from political life. Many blamed this ban for the state of affairs in the South as Reconstruction moved toward its end.

With many Republicans moving back north, the South was unstable and full of corruption in its state governments.

In addition to these factors, the Panic of 1873 triggered an economic depression, and Northerners no longer found it profitable to be guardians for the ex-slaves. It seemed that the economy had to take center stage for everyone to get the nation back on an even financial keel.

As the economy declined, the Stalwart Republicans replaced the Radical Republicans. The country was bone-weary from the political and physical violence of the Reconstruction. These Republicans were not interested in controlling or punishing the South anymore. They were concerned with the economy, corruption in public life, and trade. Over the years, the Radical Republicans had become leaderless, and they drifted apart as different factions arose. This had opened the door for the Stalwart Republicans, of which many former Radical Republicans joined the ranks, as they wanted to take a more cautious approach to politics.

The Democrats also changed. Dubbing themselves the Redeemers, the New Departure Democrats moved away from the pro-slavery Democrats and the former Copperheads. The Copperheads had been Democrats who opposed the Civil War and wanted a peace settlement made with the Confederates. They dissolved in 1868, shortly after the war ended. The New Departure Democrats were also focused on the economy, business, trade, and corruption, particularly in the Southern governments. Their goals meshed well with the changes in the Republican Party. These Democrats gained home rule in the South and declared that the best government was a local government. For Southerners, this meant an all-white government, with no room for ex-slaves or even white Republicans. With these policies in place, Reconstruction ended in some Southern states, such as Virginia, Tennessee, and Georgia.

The Depression of 1873 lasted for six years and destroyed the last vestiges of Northern interest in the Reconstruction. In both the North and the South, the depression hit hard. Labor unions died out, and Southerners lost their farms and land. Wages fell, and debt and bankruptcies grew all over the country. The Democrats used this environment to take control of the House of Representatives in 1874, doing so for the first time since the Civil War began.

It was easier for the Democrats to gain control during this time because of all the corruption going on in Grant's administration. The most well-known incident was the Whiskey Ring in 1875, in which government officials stole millions of dollars in a tax evasion scam. But there were problems before this. In 1869, Grant was tied to the Black Friday scandal, in which speculators became close to Grant and learned inside secrets, manipulating the market and ruining the economy. This scandal was not the sole reason for the Panic of 1873, but it did contribute to it. These scandals led the public to distrust Grant and, in turn, the Republicans.

Because of these changes in the political environment, the Reconstruction officially ended when President Rutherford B. Hayes withdrew all Union troops from the Southern states of North Carolina, Florida, and Louisiana after assuming office. From here on, the promises of the Radical Reconstruction fell by the wayside, and the Reconstruction officially died. Unfortunately, the violence and discrimination in the South meant most blacks couldn't vote, and few held public office. In the decades that followed the end of Reconstruction, blacks faced even worse hardships and discrimination. It would take until the 1960s for any of that to truly change.

Chapter 16 – After the Reconstruction

The end of the Reconstruction era came abruptly after the Compromise of 1877. To many, though, the Reconstruction seemed to stagger to its death.

The period that followed the end of the Reconstruction was deemed "the Redemption" by white Southerners. This period was certainly not geared toward the black residents of the South. Democratic local and state governments were finally free to organize life in the South the way they wanted it. And they wanted segregation and discrimination.

The Jim Crow Laws

The new Democratic state governments across the South passed a variety of Jim Crow laws. Much like the earlier Black Codes, the Jim Crow laws were meant to incarcerate and segregate blacks as much as possible and keep them from voting.

But who was Jim Crow? It is believed that there was never actually a person named this. The name came from a song and dance routine, which was created before the Civil War even broke out. It has been thought that the name Jim Crow came from a man named Jim Cuff (although it's possible his name was actually Jim Crow), who was a disabled slave. The song was meant to be entertaining, but it mocked black people, especially as the song and dance was performed by a white man in black face. Around 1840, the term "Jim Crow" was used to refer to black people, and white politicians simply adopted the name after the Reconstruction era had ended.

The Jim Crow laws were responsible for the segregation of public facilities and institutions. These included schools, theaters, public bathrooms, and water fountains, just to name a few. This means there was two of everything, as there needed to be one for whites and one for blacks. Although it seemed as if the South was upholding the future ruling of *Plessy v. Ferguson* ("separate but equal"), that wasn't the case. The black facilities were far less in quality than the white facilities. African Americans were targeted by whites for minor infractions, and the laws often didn't look kindly in their favor, even if they were in the right. Blacks couldn't vote, serve on juries, or hold public office. In other words, things were certainly not "separate but equal." The next chapter will discuss the Supreme Court decision of *Plessy v. Ferguson* in more detail, but it was a monumental case that took place in 1896, about twenty years after Reconstruction had ended. This doctrine held sway for decades until the civil rights movement of the 1950s and 1960s. It should also be noted that these laws could be found elsewhere in the United States, but they were primarily focused, as well as harsher, in the South.

In Louisiana, in 1900, the black community was the largest population group in the state. Yet less than 5,500 were in the voter registration books. This continued to decrease until there were only 730 registered African Americans. In North Carolina, from 1896 to 1904, the black community was completely purged from the voter rolls. Black people were essentially invisible within the political system. Since you had to be a registered voter to run for office or serve on a jury, this meant blacks were excluded from doing these things. Not having African Americans in office meant blacks had no voice as far as politics were concerned. And not having blacks on juries often meant African Americans would be tried by all-white juries who could be quick to condemn based on just their skin color. It also helped to encourage whites to engage in violence against the black community, such as lynching, as they knew there would often be no repercussions for their actions.

For the most part, the courts upheld the legislation, new constitutions, and actions by the Southern states. During this time period, the complete suppression of the black vote ensured that the white Democrats would remain in control. It was a time of cruelty and oppression for black Southerners and even their white allies.

Despite all the talk in the years after Reconstruction about a new South, it remained very close to the old pre-war South. Southern blacks were free, but what did that freedom mean if you had no job, no money, no home, and no hope of changing things? Small groups of black men found work in the foundries and mills, forming iron and steel. They were banned from working in the rapidly growing textile mills. These textile mills were owned by whites, who chose to hire women and even children before hiring a black man.

The South was able to institutionalize segregation in housing, public accommodations, and public schools by 1900. When they were challenged, the Supreme Court upheld the Jim Crow laws. This legal segregation allowed whites to feel superior to "inferior blacks." The myths about black laziness, which had been around since the time of slavery but which was amplified during this time, and the institutionalization of segregation allowed for an atmosphere of violence. Lynchings became almost commonplace, along with whippings, things that would have been similar to what the slaves had endured.

Because the Southern white establishment feared the African Americans banding together and taking charge (which, if they had been able to do so, they would have been able to take the reins of power quite easily as they outnumbered the whites), they looked for ways to deny African Americans their voting rights. This was where poll taxes and literacy tests came into play. If you recall, these types of tactics were intentionally left out of the Fourteenth Amendment.

An excellent example of the situation blacks found themselves in was in Mississippi in 1890. The state constitution placed limits on voting rights, which included excluding anyone who had been convicted of a crime (including vagrancy), residency requirements, poll taxes and payment of all other taxes, and the infamous literacy test. These were all enshrined in the Mississippi Constitution.

There were, of course, loopholes designed so poor and uneducated whites could be able to vote. These were the grandfather clauses that allowed anyone whose ancestors had been registered to be registered as well. Another example of a loophole can be seen in those white people who couldn't read. They would be allowed to vote if they could show that they understood the Constitution. Eventually, the grandfather clauses were stripped away by the Supreme Court, but the states found other ways to prevent blacks from voting.

The Black Community after Reconstruction

Blacks certainly had a hard life, but the people responded in different ways. Many left the South for the North, while a few went to Africa. In some states, blacks were able to establish their own towns, which were composed entirely of African Americans. These were primarily in Kansas, Oklahoma, and Tennessee. Some organized or were a part of movements like the National Afro-American League (1890–1908).

There were great differences in the black community about the best way to reclaim their civil rights. Two men, W. E. B. Du Bois and Booker T. Washington, best personify these differences. Washington was the founder of the Tuskegee Institute, in addition to being an author and advisor, while Du Bois was a philosopher, sociologist, and writer. Washington favored a course where blacks would become independent of whites by concentrating on improving themselves within the economy. He felt the time spent challenging discrimination or fighting for equality only took away from African American economic growth. In 1903, Du Bois wrote *The Souls of Black Folks*, in which he attacked Booker T. Washington's position. Du Bois believed that education was vital and more than a trade apprenticeship. He wanted blacks to have access to every level of formal education, including higher education. He advocated for intelligent, well-educated blacks to change the system by voting where it was allowed and protesting where it was not.

Education had been expanding in these years, with the Morrill Act of 1862 creating both white and black colleges. The next Morrill Act in 1890 provided more funding for these schools and also forbade racial discrimination. Of course, the black community truly did not benefit from expanding public education until many decades later. By 1900, it is believed that over 2,000 blacks had earned higher-education degrees.

The new immigration that followed the post-war industrial rise was a slap in the face to Southern blacks, who were still locked into a segregated society. Although these immigrants faced many hardships, they were more easily accepted into the melting pot of America while blacks struggled to survive. These immigrants faced prejudice, some of which endures to this day, and this influx also brought about a short revival of the Ku Klux Klan, as they opposed immigration. Native Americans also felt immigration was overall negative in regards to their place in American society.

In general, life was not much better for non-whites in the South after the Reconstruction, and it would not get better for many decades.

Chapter 17 – Plessy v. Ferguson: Separate but Equal, 1896

Although *Plessy v. Ferguson* took place after Reconstruction, it is an excellent example of how the black civil rights movement had stunted. This was a landmark case that the Supreme Court ruled on, and their ruling on the matter would be the guiding light for decades, allowing suffering and inequities to non-whites to occur.

The year was 1896, and the question before the Supreme Court was the constitutionality of racial segregation. This was the historic case that made "separate but equal" accommodations the law of the South until the 1960s, which was when this decision was overruled. With respect to where America is now regarding racism and equality, this Supreme Court ruling might be the most influential decision the court ever made, even though it was overturned.

The plaintiff, Homer Plessy, was a resident of New Orleans. He was mixed race (he was one-eighth black, seven-eighths white). Plessy was fair-skinned, but under Louisiana law, he was considered to be black, which meant he had to adhere to the strict laws put in place for segregation. One such law had been passed in 1890. This was the Separate Car Act, which required separate accommodations on trains for white and non-white riders. In 1892, Homer deliberately broke the law while boarding a train car labeled "whites only."

On June 7th, 1892, Plessy took part in an orchestrated move to test the limits of this law, which was coordinated by the Comité des Citoyens ("Citizens' Committee"). This was a diverse group fighting against racial discrimination in a world that constantly put whites first. First, Plessy bought a ticket for a first-class seat at the Press Street Depot in New Orleans. He then boarded the whites-only car that was going to Covington, Louisiana, on the East Louisiana Railroad. The railroad had been notified in advance that Plessy intended to challenge the law. The company itself actually opposed the law because it required them to add more cars.

The Comité des Citoyens hired a private detective so he could confront and detain Plessy when he boarded the train car. The group was worried that if someone else had apprehended Plessy, he might be charged with something like vagrancy instead of being charged for violating the Separate Car Act. After Plessy took his seat in the whites-only car, the detective ordered him to get up and move to the "colored section." When he refused to do so, the private detective arrested him. He was charged with one violation of the Separate Car Act and was remanded to Orleans Parish for trial.

Plessy challenged the law under the Thirteenth and Fourteenth Amendments. He claimed he did not receive "equal treatment under the law." The presiding judge in Orleans Parish ruled that because the railroad operated within the state of Louisiana, they could regulate their company as they saw fit. Plessy was convicted and fined $25. The case was immediately appealed to the Supreme Court of Louisiana.

The Comité des Citoyens provided the lawyers to challenge the Separate Court Act to the Supreme Court of Louisiana. This court decided that the previous judge's ruling had been sound and would stand. The justices declared there had been no violation of the Fourteenth Amendment, as the court was able to cite precedents in a couple of cases in the North. For instance, the Massachusetts

Supreme Court had ruled that segregated schools were constitutional. However, this ruling took place in 1849, which was before the ratification of the Fourteenth Amendment. The Louisiana justices also spoke of another case, which came out of Pennsylvania. A law mandated separate railcars for different races, just as the New Orleans law did. In this case, the Pennsylvania Supreme Court said that having segregation in place doesn't mean one is below another. Instead, "it is simply to say that following the order of Divine Providence, human authority ought not to compel these widely separated races to intermix."

Since the Supreme Court of Louisiana failed to issue the ruling the Comité des Citoyens was searching for, the group appealed to the United States Supreme Court. This was the plan all along, as the committee hoped to have segregation declared unconstitutional throughout the entire country.

The Supreme Court agreed to hear the case, and it was added to the docket in 1896. Two separate legal briefs for Plessy were submitted to the court by Albion W. Tourgée and Samuel F. Phillips. Tourgée was considered to be the most outspoken white Republican in the nation on the issue of equality. He was an instrumental member of the Comité des Citoyens; in fact, he was the one to suggest that the man who boarded the train be fairer-skinned. Both gentlemen testified for Plessy at the Supreme Court hearing, although Tourgée played a larger role in the case. They claimed that Plessy had rights under the Thirteenth and Fourteenth Amendments, which were violated by the Separate Car Act. They argued that the Equal Protection Clause guarantees the same rights to all United States citizens. Tourgée also argued that since the reputation of black men was as slaves or property, they were considered to be inferior and given poorer separate accommodations.

Attorney General Milton Joseph Cunningham wrote the state's legal brief. He was known for his efforts to restore white supremacy. In fact, Cunningham worked so vigorously in restoring white supremacy in the South that he was eventually arrested himself for violating laws.

Following these oral arguments, the justices took the case under review. They issued their decision on May 18th, 1896. What had begun as a "test case" (cases that bring clarity to certain laws) came to a resolution almost four years later. By a seven to one vote, the Supreme Court rejected Plessy's arguments and ruled for the defendant. The court upheld the Separate Car Act as constitutional.

Only eight justices took part in this decision because one of the justices, Justice David J. Brewer, had missed the oral arguments due to the death of his daughter and was thus recused from the decision-making process. Justice Henry Billings Brown wrote the majority opinion, which first looked at the Thirteenth Amendment. The Supreme Court decided that this law had not violated it, as the majority of justices interpreted the Thirteenth Amendment as providing the necessary amount of equality to abolish slavery. The Thirteenth Amendment did not bestow any other legal equality.

The Supreme Court opinion then turned toward the arguments around the Fourteenth Amendment and the Equal Protection Clause. This clause says, "nor shall any State...deny to any person within its jurisdiction the equal protection of the laws." The court's decision was that the Fourteenth Amendment, while guaranteeing legal equality, did not intend to ban other types of discrimination. In other words, the amendment did not abolish the differences between the races, and it also did not intend for "a commingling of the races upon terms unsatisfactory to either."

The Supreme Court decided that racial separation laws were well within the purview of the state of Louisiana. The court believed that as long as a law was reasonable and was not intended to oppress another, it would remain legal. However, the real question regarding segregation laws was whether or not the law was reasonable. The court believed that the state should have discretionary authority over what was reasonable.

The Supreme Court rejected the argument that segregation dehumanized the black race, saying, "We consider the underlying fallacy of the plaintiff's argument to consist in the assumption that the enforced separation of the two races stamps the colored race with a badge of inferiority. If this be so, it is not by reason of anything found in the act, but solely because the colored race chooses to put that construction on it." With this move, the US Supreme Court declared that "separate but equal" accommodations were certainly constitutional.

Only one justice dissented from this opinion, and he did so with an elegance and grace that has held up under historical scrutiny. John Marshall Harlan believed that the Louisiana law implied that blacks were inferior. In his eloquent dissent, Harlan wrote, "But in view of the Constitution, in the eye of the law, there is in this country no superior, dominant, ruling class of citizens. There is no caste here. Our Constitution is color-blind, and neither knows nor tolerates classes among citizens. In respect of civil rights, all citizens are equal before the law. The humblest is the peer of the most powerful. The law regards man as man, and takes no account of his surroundings or of his color when his civil rights as guaranteed by the supreme law of the land are involved...Everyone knows that the statute in question had its origin in the purpose, not so much to exclude white people from railroad cars occupied by blacks, as to exclude people of color from coaches occupied by or assigned to white persons...Under the guise of giving equal accommodation for whites and blacks, the law sought to compel the latter to keep to themselves while traveling in railroad passenger coaches. No one would be so wanting in candor as to assert the contrary."

Harlan then proposed that this decision would go down in history as one of the worst decisions the Supreme Court ever made. And Harlan was right. Time and time again, scholars have come to the same conclusion that the *Dred Scott v. Sandford* and the *Plessy v. Ferguson* decisions are at the top of the Supreme Court's worst rulings. This decision in *Plessy v. Ferguson* institutionalized segregation in the South for decades to come.

This Supreme Court decision erased all the positive legislative gains of the Radical Reconstruction era. "Separate but equal" became the doctrine of the land, and future Supreme Court cases only strengthened it.

Everyone knows now that the accommodations offered to people of color in this time period were indeed separate, but they were certainly not equal. One of the most significant impacts was in the realm of public schools. Even before this decision by the Supreme Court, funding for white and black schools was significantly unequal. Black schools were typically old, substandard buildings. They were underfunded, and their supplies and textbooks were old and used. In 1927, the US Supreme Court ruled in *Lum v. Rice* that public schools in Mississippi could completely ban Chinese American children from attending white schools. Since going to school was compulsory, the Supreme Court ruled that Lum could choose to attend a private school or attend schools with other minorities.

When blacks began to migrate again to the North to enjoy more equality, segregation and Jim Crow laws simply followed them. Amusement parks and swimming pools in states like Indiana were whites-only well into the 1950s. Oftentimes in the North, segregation was not the law but rather an unspoken expectation.

Plessy v. Ferguson also allowed states throughout the South to prevent people of color from registering and voting. The state's legislatures put more obstacles in place beyond the literacy tests and poll taxes. For example, some states required one to be a property owner in order to vote.

In 1954, the US Supreme Court in *Brown v. Board of Education* declared that segregation in public schools was not equal and was unconstitutional. *Plessy v. Ferguson* was no longer the precedent on segregation issues, even though it was never explicitly overturned.

Finally, in 1964, the Civil Rights Act outlawed any form of segregation. The Voting Rights Act of 1965 put the federal government back into an oversight and enforcement role with respect to registering and voting.

In 2009, Keith Plessy and Phoebe Ferguson, descendants of the original plaintiff and defendant in the 1896 case, joined together to form the Plessy and Ferguson Foundation for Education and Reconciliation. This foundation aims to teach the true history of the civil rights struggle in the United States. They use art, film, and other public programs to let others understand *Plessy v. Ferguson* and its impact over the years.

For those interested in viewing history firsthand, a marker has been placed at the corner of Press and Royal Streets in Louisiana, recognizing the place where Plessy boarded that whites-only train car all those years ago.

Afterword: The Legacy of Reconstruction and Today's Civil Rights Issues

As we look at the political and social climate in the United States in the early 20th century, we might be fooled into believing that we have left the Civil War and its Reconstruction far behind us. After all, the civil rights movement of the 1960s resulted in new legislation and voting rights. Today, blacks and whites work together, live in the same neighborhoods, and socialize together. On the outside, it appears as if systemic racism is a relic of the past.

However, the year 2020 heard cries from the black community, whose voices were raised, yet again, in the name of social justice and equality. This is a highly contentious topic in the United States today, but it is important to examine why the African American community feels this way, especially as it relates directly to what was set in place during Reconstruction. Blacks continue to outnumber whites in prisons, although the number between the two has been steadily decreasing over the years. And although white people have the highest mortality rate when it comes to police violence, one has to keep in mind that there are more white people than black people in the

United States, which means that black people suffer more in this sphere as well. In addition to this, blacks also face worsening voter rights. In 2013, the US Supreme Court struck down two provisions of the Voting Rights Act of 1965, one of which had required local and state governments to obtain federal approval before changing voting laws. Since then, nearly 1,000 polling places have been closed, with the majority of these in predominately African American districts. Many have also felt that stricter voter ID laws and rules regarding mail-in or absentee ballots are symptoms of the same racial disease the country has suffered from since its inception. To be fair, many people believe these types of laws are not racist but are simply intended to prevent voter fraud or to decrease government spending, but it can be hard to determine where the line between the two starts and ends. Regardless of the differences in opinion, there is still a divide in the United States today.

We will leave you with some final questions, questions that scholars are still trying to answer today. Was the Reconstruction successful, or did it only perpetuate systemic racism in the nation? And was there ever really a chance to get beyond the hurt and bitterness caused by the Civil War?

Here's another book by Captivating History that you might like

Free Bonus from Captivating History (Available for a Limited time)

Hi History Lovers!

Now you have a chance to join our exclusive history list so you can get your first history ebook for free as well as discounts and a potential to get more history books for free! Simply visit the link below to join.

Captivatinghistory.com/ebook

Also, make sure to follow us on Facebook, Twitter and Youtube by searching for Captivating History.

References

Online Sites:

Antebellum era | Project Gutenberg Self-Publishing - eBooks | Read eBooks online. Dec. 9, 2020

Radical Reconstruction, 1867–1872 | US History II (OS Collection) (lumenlearning.com). Dec. 9, 2020.

Confederate railroads in the American Civil War - Wikipedia. Dec. 18, 2020.

Presidency of Andrew Johnson - Wikipedia. Dec. 21, 2020.

Question: What was the amount of South Carolina's Debt at the End of the Civil War? | Civil War History Discussion (civilwartalk.com). Dec. 18, 2020.

Those Southern Repudiated Bonds | VQR Online. Dec. 18, 2020.

The Wade-Davis Bill and Reconstruction (thoughtco.com). Dec 21, 2020.

Reconstruction and Rights | Civil War and Reconstruction, 1861-1877 | U.S. History Primary Source Timeline | Classroom Materials at the Library of Congress | Library of Congress (loc.gov). Dec. 10, 2020.

Civil Rights Act of 1866 - Wikipedia. Dec. 16, 2020.

Voting Rights Act of 1965 - Definition, Summary & Significance - HISTORY. Dec. 18, 2020.

Joint Committee on Reconstruction - Bing. Dec. 16, 2020.

Jim Crow Laws: Definition, Facts & Timeline - HISTORY. Dec. 11, 2020.

Radical Reconstruction | History, Causes, & Effects | Britannica. Dec. 10, 2020.

Black Codes (United States) - Wikipedia. Dec. 9, 2020.

Andrew Johnson, Impeachment, and Reconstruction – Brewminate. Dec. 18, 2020.

How did the South react to the election of Abraham Lincoln as President of the U.S. in 1860? - eNotes.com. Dec. 9, 2020.

Reconstruction - Civil War End, Changes & Act of 1867 - HISTORY. Dec. 10, 2020.

U.S. Constitution - Thirteenth Amendment | Resources | Constitution Annotated | Congress.gov | Library of Congress. Dec. 17, 2020.

Freedmen's Bureau - Wikipedia. Dec 17, 2020.

How the 1876 Election Tested the Constitution and Effectively Ended Reconstruction - HISTORY. Dec. 21, 2020.

Civil War - Causes, Dates & Battles - HISTORY. Dec. 11, 2020.

Books and Publications

Foner, Eric. *Reconstruction Updated Edition: America's Unfinished Revolution, 1863-18* (Harper Perennial Modern Classics). Format: Kindle Edition, Amazon. December 2, 2014.

Gates, Henry Louis Jr. *Stony the Road: Reconstruction, White Supremacy, and the Rise of Jim Crow.* Format: Kindle Edition. April 2, 2019.

Simpson, Brooks D. *Reconstruction: Voices from America's First Great Struggle for Racial Equality* (LOA #303) (Library of America). Format: Kindle Edition, Amazon. January 30, 2018.